CW00821882

Stand The F*ck Out

The No-Nonsense Guide to Positioning
a Business, Finding the Right People,
and Building a Durable Brand

Louis Grenier

STAND THE F*CK OUT

The No-Nonsense Guide to Positioning Your Business, Finding Your People, and Building a Durable Brand

LOUIS GRENIER

Foreword by Joe Pulizzi

Copyright © by 2024 Louis Grenier

All rights reserved. No part of this publication may be reproduced, distributed, or transmitted in any form or by any means, including photocopying, recording, or other electronic or mechanical methods, without the prior written permission of the publisher, except in the case of brief quotations embodied in critical reviews and certain other noncommercial uses permitted by copyright law.

ISBN: 979-8-9898626-0-3

Tilt Publishing
700 Park Offices Drive, Suite 250
Research Triangle, NC 27709

Table of Contents

Who the F*ck Is This Guy? A Foreword by Joe Pulizzi

I've written forewords for over 20 different authors.

So when Louis asked me to write the foreword for his book, I wasn't surprised.

I like what Louis is doing. I've been on his podcast. I've been following his writings on LinkedIn. And then I read this book.

So I said yes . . . And I knew I had to step up my game.

I spent hours crafting a message about differentiation. About how marketers need to listen to Louis and stand the f*ck out.

I finished and was generally happy with my work.

On May 1st, I emailed it to him.

"Edit at will. I hope you like it.—JP"

Then, nothing.

Nothing on day two.

Nothing on day five.

On May 9th, I followed up.

"Did this work for you?"

Louis emailed me back 14 minutes later.

This foreword would be perfect for most marketing books but . . . does it stand the f*ck out?

I know it may sound cheeky coming from someone who hasn't accomplished 1 percent of what you have, but (1) I didn't feel your personality come through, (2) it needs to slap more, maybe with a story? How did you come across my stuff? Or something else entirely?, and (3) I never read forewords and I suspect most of my readers won't either . . . Unless we make it so good, they have to read it.

My initial thought:

Who the f*ck is this guy? What the f*ck does he know about writing a foreword? What does he know about writing a book, for that matter?

Five hours later, I started writing this story.

After this experience, I wondered how many people didn't tell me the truth about my writing, branding, or whatever. I thought about all the marketing programs I was a part of. Did I really do my best? Or did I hold something back?

I think most people in marketing just blindly accept whatever they are given. They don't rock the boat. They don't get challenged to be better. To do better. They probably don't have any sarcastic Frenchmen around to force them to think and be different.

Liberté, Égalité, Fraternité

I'm honestly still pissed as I write this. When someone criticizes you, it's not easy to take. You want to deflect. You want to take that emotion and create a laser of hatred the other way.

Or . . . you could listen to that advice and redirect it into something amazing. Something that stands the f*ck out.

So, you and I. We need to step up our game if we want to stand the f*ck out.

And this book will do it.

Read it, and stop making excuses about why things just aren't working out for you.

By the end of this book, you probably won't like Louis either, but you'll thank him for it.

Oh, and Louis . . . f*ck you.

Joe Pulizzi
Author of five bestselling but mediocre marketing books

Ever Feel Like . . . ?

Jonathan Goodman (Figure I.1) is the CEO of the PTDC (Personal Trainer Development Center), an education business that has trained more than 250,000+ fitness trainers and nutrition coaches.[1] He also happens to have my dream body (but don't tell him that, please).

Figure I.1. Jon Goodman looking cool. (Photograph by Taryn Baxter, 2019.)

When we met through a mutual friend, Jon's business was stuck: "We don't have a clear and focused direction. We're all over the place and tend to jump on whatever tactic seems to work for others instead of defining

---

1   Learn more about Jonathan Goodman and the PTDC here: https://www.theptdc.com/about.

and sticking to our positioning." Worse, post-Covid boom, their revenue had flatlined.

I was so surprised. Not by the business plateau, which is common, but by Jon and his team looking like deer in headlights. These people weren't rookies. We're talking about a guy with 11 books published, 250,000+ sales, a blog with more than 1,500 articles, and a team of brainboxes who train others in marketing. Nice people, too.

What the fuck was going on? They had plenty of stats on their customer demographics, strategy docs, messaging frameworks—you name it. On paper, they had their shit together.

But in reality? They were neck-deep in marketing bullshit: overwhelmed, triple-guessing themselves and convinced they were missing some sort of magic trick. They went as far as copying their bigger rivals' intense, discount-heavy communications. And yet, deep down, they believed they were here to make real, lasting changes in people's lives—not selling shortcuts or false promises. It was like watching a couple clinging to a dead marriage "for the kids," you know?

Have You Experienced Something Similar? You Know What I'm Talking About

The constant pressure caused by those *you're-just-one-funnel-away* gurus. The "secrets" all your competitors know already (except you!). The new artificial intelligence (AI) tools that will 100x your business while you're sleeping with almost no detectable brain activity. The FOMO (fear of missing out) bullshit like, "Marketing is moving so fast, you have to keep up! It's changing all the time!"

They make you wonder, *Wait . . . am I missing something? Or am I just fucking stupid? Should I just quit everything and start a goat farm?* They chip away at your confidence, self-worth, and joy in what you do . . . leaving you feeling useless. And that's when they suck you into craving the quick fixes they peddle.

But here's the thing: you *don't* have to play that game. Just like Jon and the PTDC, you *must* stand the f*ck out, yes, but on your own terms. You deserve to feel confident in your abilities without selling your soul. You deserve to build a brand that truly reflects who you *really* are without copying competitors. You deserve to attract the right people and have fun in the process.

> Look, if you had one shot or one opportunity
> To seize everything you ever wanted in one moment
> Would you capture it or just let it slip?
> Yo[2]

Yo, indeed.

2 Eminem. 2015. "Lose Yourself." YouTube. https://www.youtube.com/watch?v=_Yhyp-_hX2s.

Enter: The Stand The F*ck Out (STFO) Methodology

Stand The F*ck Out (STFO) is a no-nonsense marketing methodology designed to help businesses find their unique positioning, build a distinctive brand, and reach their ideal customers—all without falling prey to marketing bullshit. It's the guide I wish I had when I started my career as a naive "digital marketing enthusiast," burned through $20k in savings launching my first agency, or nearly got the sack from my dream job at a bootstrapped tech start-up. Unlike most positioning, branding, and lead generation advice:

- **It's actionable.** There's some theory, of course, but you'll find practical exercises you can use *right away* alongside real examples from all kinds of businesses—big or small, B2C, B2B, B2B2C2C2B2C, and even personal brands.

- **It's simple.** Simplicity is underrated; complexity is fake-smart.[3] I've made it easy to understand and implement—even if you think you couldn't market a fresh croissant to someone starving in a boulangerie.

- **It's fun.** I'm sick to death of the borefest in marketing circles. Life is short; might as well have some fun, right? I hope the examples,

---

3   Thank you Peep Laja for this gem: https://www.linkedin.com/posts/peeplaja_simplicity-is-underrated-complexity-is-fake-smart-activity-7044264908229677056-Ns_D/.

drawings, and other bits will make you forget, at least for a fleeting moment, that we're on a rock traveling around a giant burning star at approximately 107,000 km/h.

This methodology has been years in the making. It began as a course idea for the 2,000 followers I had from my marketing agency in Dublin. Twelve people signed up, earning me $6,000—the most I'd ever made online. I used their feedback to refine the course. I also used information from hundreds of podcast interviews (shown in Figure I.2) from my podcast *Everyone Hates Marketers*, along with books, research papers, and other lovely stuff. Then I moved on to one-on-one coaching and team sessions for a few years. After that, I felt ready to begin working on the book.

Figure I.2. Photo of the printed transcripts of interviews and my notes.

Once I finished the shitty first draft, I invited 70 marketers and business owners to rip it apart. This was *by far* the most frightening yet valuable thing I ever did in my career. Without their 5,000 comments and reactions (!) across three versions of the manuscript, this book would have been . . . shit.

While I cannot promise STFO is going to skyrocket your business and launch it into hyper-mega-giga-growth, I can promise the following:

- **Keep reading for a few minutes, and you'll feel *relief*.** Because you're *not* the only one feeling like you're not good at this marketing thing. You're *not* the only one who's scared of fucking it up. None of this is your fault, and I will show you why.

- **Read the book once, and the foggy shit is going to clear.** You'll know what to do, what *not* to do, and where to spend your time and money for maximum *bonanza*.

- **Apply the methodology in real life, and you'll become unstoppable—no matter what shit is thrown at you.** You'll have the tools to handle anything and the results to prove it. Work will become satisfying again.

This mirrors the PTDC team's journey after we started working together. After our first workshop, they realized they *weren't* missing any secret marketing tricks (the relief!). After a few more weeks, we worked through the four stages of the methodology, which gave them a clear, simple plan to follow. That's when the fog lifted. Within a month, their confidence grew. Jon came out of hiding and (re)became the face of the brand, growing his online following to over 200,000. More importantly, this strategy turned their struggling company around, leading to nearly $2 million in profit within a year.

Is This Book for You?

The ones who need the methodology the most and will get the most from it are:

- **Marketing business owners.** You want to grow your creative business and help your clients stand the f*ck out. I'm loosely using the term "creative business" to include ad/digital/social media agencies, PR firms, consulting practices, and so on.

- **Marketing executives.** You're working in a high-pressure environment where you're expected to deliver much more with far less. You must prove your worth to shareholders, bosses, or teammates, almost every day.

- **Reluctant marketers.** You're a creator, founder, or small business owner who didn't set out to be a marketer. Yet you find yourself creating a "lead magnet" to grow your email list, maintaining a content calendar for your "socials," and learning copywriting from a 19-year-old YouTuber.

But please don't put the book down if you don't fit neatly into these categories. Over the years I've seen this methodology benefit gelato makers in Saudi Arabia, physiotherapists in Québec, and real estate agents in Ireland. So, in short, if you have a conscience, want to grow your business, and feel overwhelmed by marketing bullshit, I hope you'll still give it a go.

Now let's get down into the weeds a bit more.

The Methodology Has Four Stages

It's really a step-by-step guide (see Figure I.3) and it all starts with **insight foraging**, where you dig deep to uncover what makes your customers tick. Then you'll use **unique positioning** to give people a damn good reason to choose you over the rest. With a **distinctive brand**, you'll make sure you're impossible to forget, even if people aren't ready to buy right now. And finally, **continuous reach** keeps the right people coming back for more while drawing new ones in.

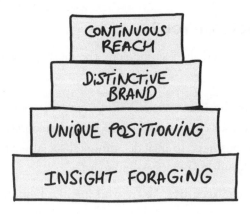

Figure I.3. The four stages of Stand The F*ck Out.

Stage 1. Insight Foraging

To stand the f*ck out, we start by digging for the raw, unfiltered truths about your customers—the kind of insights your competitors wouldn't know where to find. You'll use these insights to answer the questions plaguing many others: What to sell? Whom to focus on? What sets us apart? How to get better leads? Why should people care?

With **insight foraging**, the goal is to uncover the hidden truths about your customers. It's about getting your hands dirty and unearthing the insights that will become the foundation of your quest to stand the f*ck out.

Stage 2. Unique Positioning

A gazillion other brands are screaming, "We're the best!" through megaphones pointed to microphones attached to amps set to 11. How are you supposed to stand the f*ck out so the right people choose you?

With a **unique positioning**, you give the right people a compelling reason to choose you. It's about finding specific problems that the competition has overlooked. This is where you may find new market space and how you can win as an underdog.

Stage 3. Distinctive Brand

You can have the most **unique positioning** from the Pyrenees to the Alps, but if no one has ever heard of you it doesn't matter. And even if people pay attention to you, they may not be ready to buy right now.

With a **distinctive brand**, you'll boost your odds of being noticed, sticking in people's minds, and ending up on their shortlist when they're ready to buy—all without resorting to ridiculous stunts like dancing naked with a pineapple on your head.

Stage 4. Continuous Reach

And finally, you can't just rely on your current fans and their loyalty. People's lives change—they move, switch jobs, or their needs evolve. That's why you need a constant flow of new customers.

Continuous reach means getting in front of the right people at the right time with the right stuff, as often as your budget allows. This consistent visibility keeps you top-of-mind, so you're more likely to be picked when they're ready to buy.

OK, that's all you need to know for now.

Ready to stand the f*ck out?

Cool, I'll see you in Stage 1.

Insight Foraging

I'm from France originally (what do you mean you already knew?!). More precisely, I'm from a small town near Clermont-Ferrand, which is next to a chain of extinct volcanoes.

While I was growing up there, one of my favorite things to do was go with my dad and his best friend (we called him "Pinoche") to hunt for cèpe mushrooms (also known as porcini). We would wake up super early, head over to one of their favorite hunting spots, and walk through the oak woods for hours.

It was fun because:

- **We didn't know where the mushrooms would be.** While Pinoche knew a couple of secret spots, there was no guarantee we'd find anything there.

- **We weren't sure if the mushroom we saw behind that fallen log was edible or poisonous**—or if we had just been tricked by a bunch of leaves.

- **We knew there was no point following other mycologists around.** Just because someone else found a great spot didn't mean we'd have the same luck.

- **We understood that the journey mattered as much as the mushrooms themselves.** Finding those juicy fungi was great, but spending time in nature together was equally important.

The first step on your quest to stand the f*ck out works in a similar way, but **instead of hunting for mushrooms, you will be hunting for juicy** *insights* **(see Figure S1.1).**

*Figure S1.1. Juicy insights are the foundation of the Stand The F*ck Out framework.*

1

The Poisonous Insights

I seduced my wife with food.

She's always been picky, so when we were dating I made it my mission to find a simple meal she would love. I zeroed in on a mushroom risotto (*risotto ai funghi*): arborio short-grain rice, fresh porcini mushrooms, white wine, broth, and Parmesan cheese.

Now let me paint you two scenarios.

Scenario 1. I quickly read through a recipe online, then rush to the local supermarket. I grab the saddest canned button mushrooms—*I mean, who cares? It's just mushrooms.* I snatch some random cheese and the first packet of white rice I see. *How difficult could making this dish be? There are just, like, five ingredients.* I throw them all into a pan and wish for the best.

Scenario 2. The day before our date, I'm exploring the forest like a truffle-hunting pig, looking for juicy porcini mushrooms. I sweet-talk the local cheesemonger into selling his finest Parmigiano-Reggiano. I visit the off-license next door in search of a decent Pinot Grigio wine. Back at home, I practice, I taste, I adjust. Tomorrow's date must be perfect.

OK, which scenario would lead to another date? And which would have me ghosted? I'm not going to patronize you—we both know the answer.

The more you care about sourcing quality ingredients and making your risotto, the better it'll be. It's the difference between a dish she'll always remember (and wanting another date) and one she'll forget (and I never see her again).

The Problem: Juicy Insights Are Hard to Find

It's the same thing with standing the f*ck out as a business. **The more you rely on prepackaged, generic insights all your competitors have in their possession (such as trend reports, web analytics overviews, or the 12 fictional personas created in a boardroom yesterday) the more likely you are to blend the f*ck in.**

On the other hand, **the more you care about sourcing quality insights (such as mining online reviews or running interviews) and assembling them, the more likely you are to stand the f*ck out.**

But what does hunting for **insights** actually mean? And what is an **insight**, anyway?

> **Simply put, an insight is a specific piece of information gleaned directly or indirectly from customers.** It gives you a *nuanced* understanding of why customers do what they do. When pieced together, these insights answer crucial questions about your business, such as: *What should I sell? Whom should I focus on? What makes my business unique? How can I attract better leads? Why should people care?*

The real magic of **insight foraging** is that it gives you *unshakable* confidence. You know what I mean—the kind of confidence that comes from knowing that:

- **You're *always* on the right track,** no matter what curveball gets thrown at you.

- **You're not missing *anything* crucial,** no matter what the gurus say.

- **You don't need to be some kind of creative genius to make it work,** no matter how much your brain is trying to bring you down.

All you need is a set of juicy insights. I believe hunting for market insights is as challenging as hunting for porcini mushrooms:

- **You never know where those juicy insights are hiding.** You might think you know your customers well, but you could end up empty-handed without a good process.

- **You can't rush to collect any type of insight, just like you wouldn't eat any mushroom you find in the forest.** Nausea, stomach cramps, and diarrhea are not fun for anyone—not to mention sudden death and an embarrassing obituary.[4] You must avoid rushing to make decisions based on misleading or inaccurate information.

- **Don't mindlessly follow your competitors hoping they'll lead you to new insights.** They're likely just as lost as you are, and you'll find only what they've *already* found.

- **The journey of insight hunting is as valuable as the insights themselves.** The heavyweights in your field think they know it all, but as an underdog you can uncover the nuanced details they miss. Getting close to the ground gives you a real edge.

Yes, the right insight is hard to find. There are many pitfalls to avoid. But that is what's making this activity so valuable. While I can't spend time with you in the wild to forage for insights, I can guide you to increase your

---

4   Thank you Lianna Patch for suggesting this one.

chances of finding juicy insights, which, in turn, will increase your chances of standing the f*ck out:

Get your mushroom foraging basket, your pocket knife, and some snacks. We're going out.

The Solution: Avoid Poisonous Insights at All Costs

I've spent the last decade knee-deep in customer research for businesses ranging from local retailers to big tech companies, conducting hundreds of interviews, sifting through thousands of survey responses, and training countless marketers. If I had to extract one lesson—and one only—it'd be this:

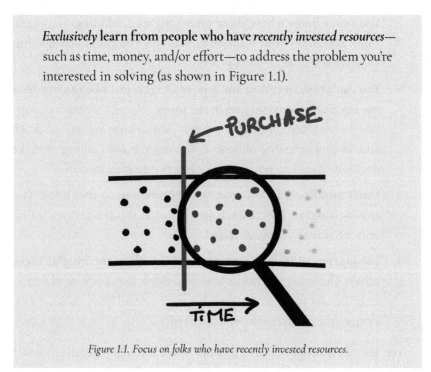

Exclusively learn from people who have *recently invested resources*— such as time, money, and/or effort—to address the problem you're interested in solving (as shown in Figure 1.1).

Figure 1.1. Focus on folks who have recently invested resources.

Why? Because those individuals are much more likely to share information that is usable since (1) you have proof they've done something you can learn from (instead of making shit up because they just don't know what the future holds), and (2) their recent behavior means it's easier for them to recall what happened.

If you don't exclusively learn from them, you may pick up poisonous insights. A **poisonous insight** is a piece of customer information that *appears* insightful on the surface but leads to harmful consequences.

For example, send a survey to the wrong people—say, folks who never bought from you—ask them the wrong questions—for example, something about future behavior—and you'll end up with **insights** that are just as good as Nostradamus's.[5] Those **poisonous insights** would make your entire risotto inedible and lead to terrible decisions like spending months, if not years, building solutions people don't really want to buy, investing shit tons of money in marketing campaigns that don't move the needle, or burning out running your business like swimming against the current.

As an underdog, you don't have the luxury of wasting energy on **poisonous insights**. You need to be efficient. Lean. Focused. To do so, pay attention to **folks who have *recently* invested resources to make progress,** mainly:

- **Your recent customers (or clients).** Those folks tend to be the greatest source of insights. Don't worry if you have none because you're just starting out (or you don't have access to them). There are other ways to collect juicy insights, which I'll cover in depth in the next chapters.

- **Recent customers of direct/indirect competitors.** You can get loads of info from them without committing industrial espionage. I'll show you how shortly.

- **Recent customers of the category/industry you're in.** This is also a great group of people to tap into, even if they don't seem connected to what you do.

At the opposite end of the spectrum, there are two types of people to avoid at all costs:

---

5   Nostradamus was a French astrologer who loved to predict the future—but very often failed at it.

Individuals Who *Appear* Interested in a Solution but *Haven't* Committed Any Resources

They're window shoppers. They *seem* like they could be your customers, they *seem* to have problems you can solve, and they are willing to help, but—this is critical—they have not yet invested their money, effort, or time into it. In other words, they're well-intentioned, but since they didn't travel down that road, they will have to make shit up to make themselves look good and/or please you.

You can spot window shoppers in a few ways. They might seem interested in what you offer, maybe even talking to sales or asking about pricing. They might tell you how they'd use your product or service, even going so far as to propose a "mutually benefiting" partnership. They might even seem ready to buy. But then . . . they vanish.

Example:

In one of my favorite interviews[6] on my podcast, *Everyone Hates Marketers,* I challenged conversion copywriter Joanna Wiebe to figure out how to write compelling copy for a fictional museum dedicated to *The Simpsons.*

Her first step? "We'd probably interview hardcore Simpsons fanatics who like visiting museums." She naturally zeroed in on a group of people who already spend their weekends visiting museums and who also happen to love the famous animated sitcom. Investigating this group would help us unearth insights like how they got there, whom they went with, and, most importantly, what motivated them to go in the first place.

On the other hand, learning about people who say they're *thinking* about going to a museum (maybe even calling for opening hours) but never setting foot inside would lead us to unearth poisonous insights based on hypotheticals—a very dangerous game.

---

6   Louis Grenier and Joanna Wiebe. 2018. "Three Steps to Write Copy That Converts." *Everyone Hates Marketers.* https://podcast.everyonehatesmarketers.com/episodes/3-steps-to-write-copy-that-converts-with-joanna-wiebe.

Individuals Who Purchased in the Distant Past (but *Haven't* Engaged Recently)

They're dormant customers. They purchased something a long time ago and will therefore have to rely on decaying/altered memories to give you information (so, yeah, they will also make shit up).

We humans forget half of what we learn within an hour, 70 percent within a day, and 90 percent after a week.[7] So if someone bought a pack of gum at a gas station five months ago, that person probably won't remember the details. In other words, avoid relying on customers who bought from you a while ago.

As a rule of thumb, a customer is considered dormant if the last purchase has happened three months or more in the past for complex, lengthy buying processes that involve more than one person (e.g., large B2B enterprise deals). For near-instant purchases, like a pack of gum at the till, one month—let alone five—would already be way too long.

Example:

According to my order confirmation email, I bought a pack of 10 Crayola washable paint bottles precisely 12 days ago. I don't remember what made me look into it. I don't remember what made me buy it. I don't remember where I was or when it was during the day. I can only remember that I bought it for my daughter and that I picked it because it's rated 4.8/5 with more than 20,000 reviews. If Crayola were to interview me today to try to extract insights, the conversation wouldn't last very long (plus, I would probably make shit up to try to help the Crayola folks so they don't leave empty-handed).

To summarize, the most valuable insights focus on individuals who have recently invested resources (time, money, effort) in solving the problem your product addresses, as their experiences will be fresh and relevant. Table 1.1 shows examples of various situations and whether they would lead to reliable insights.

---

7   NASBA. 2017. "Dr. Art Kohn Explains How to Achieve the Optimal Learning Experience with Boosts and Bursts." NASBA Registry. https://www.nasbaregistry.org/cpe-monitor-newsletters/dr-art-kohn-explains-how-to-achieve-the-optimal-learning-experience-with-boosts-and-bursts.

Table 1.1. Identifying Reliable Insights

Context	Are they reliable insights?	Why?
An online review from a customer who bought your product last week	Yes	A recent customer of your business
An interview with someone who fits your ideal customer profile but has never purchased in your category	**No, ignore**	The person lacks real experience with your category and may provide misleading information.
A conversation with your sales team about the reasons that almost stopped customers from buying	Yes	They *almost* didn't buy but overcame objections, which is a great source of information.
A survey response from someone who bought a Snickers bar at a gas station two months ago.	**No, ignore**	The person probably won't remember it because it was a low-cost, low-consideration purchase that happened too long ago.
Field observations of customers who bought something at a gas station.	Yes	Being a fly on the wall can be a great way to gather insights about how people buy.
Advice from your Uncle Eugene on what he would do in your situation	**No, ignore**	Need I say more?
Feedback from a finance director who considered purchasing accounting software but didn't (they're just going to use what they always have)	**No, ignore**	The finance director didn't overcome the forces keeping the company from switching to your solution. So the finance director can't tell you what you really need to know.

Context	Are they reliable insights?	Why?
A glowing testimonial a customer left in exchange for a huge discount	**No, ignore**	The customer might embellish the truth to gain something.
An in-depth interview with someone who spent weeks building an automated garden watering system instead of buying a ready-made solution	Yes	The person has invested a significant amount of time building a makeshift solution to the problem you're solving.

There are three methods to learn from those individuals to extract juicy insights. We'll explore each in detail, but let's get a quick overview for now. Think of this as a sneak peek before we roll up our sleeves and get our hands dirty in the chapters to come.

Insight-Foraging Method 1. Looking at Existing Data

This method relies on existing information that's mostly underused:

- **Reviews and testimonials.** These are the places where people share their experiences about products or services. If you're in an industry where online reviews are common (like fast-moving consumer goods), reviewers can become your "free interns."[8]

- **Internal customer inputs.** Your email or phone conversations with prospects-turned-customers and current clients are packed with juicy insights. For bigger businesses, consider accessing call recordings from the sales team, customer service feedback, or old surveys—anywhere your customers have shared their unfiltered thoughts and experiences.

---

8   Louis Grenier and Ryan Kulp. 2018. "Marketing Without a Budget: Grow Your Revenue with 0 Credibility or Advertising." *Everyone Hates Marketers.* https://podcast.everyonehatesmarketers.com/episodes/marketing-without-a-budget-grow-your-revenue-with-0-credibility-or-advertising.

- **Customer-facing staff.** Salespeople, for example, possess invaluable firsthand knowledge about your customers. This extends beyond your immediate sales team. Gathering insights from salespeople in similar businesses within your category can be just as valuable.

Insight-Foraging Method 2. Gathering New Data

This method relies on extracting new information, which can lead to *major* discoveries:

- **The fly-on-the-wall technique.** Watch how customers behave in natural settings (without being a creep). If you're selling online, you can observe real users as they attempt to complete tasks on your website—this can be done in person or remotely via website session recordings.[9] For brick-and-mortar businesses, you can tag along while your customers browse, choose products, and use what they bought. Watch how they interact with your brand in their natural habitat.

- **The Sherlock Holmes approach.**[10] Join communities, online forums, or real-life conferences where customers already congregate. Then pay attention to the posts with the most views and comments to understand what resonates with them.

- **Informal conversations with customers.** Ask questions during casual interactions with customers.

- **Surveys.** Send questionnaires to customers. Ask open-ended questions and analyze responses to uncover patterns and trends.

- **Method marketing.**[11] Experience the product/service firsthand, because some things are tough to understand *without* experiencing them yourself. This is especially powerful when you're working with

---

9   I'm biased, but Hotjar is great for that.

10   As mentioned by Ross Simmonds. 2018. "Content Distribution Plan: An In-Depth Process for Driving More Traffic." *Everyone Hates Marketers.* https://podcast.everyonehatesmarketers.com/episodes/content-distribution-plan-an-in-depth-process-for-driving-more-traffic.

11   Method marketing comes from "method acting," which is when performers completely immerse themselves into the role of the character they are playing.

a new client and don't have all the insider knowledge yet. Those early days are invaluable. If you're already too familiar with the product, you could try signing up for a competitor's offering. This helps you see things with a beginner's mind and uncover insights you might otherwise miss.

- **Customer interviews.**[12] Ask questions in a controlled environment to uncover insights. This works best with recent, complex purchases where a lot was at stake (in B2B). In the next chapter, I'll walk you through the art of crafting good questions and extracting juicy insights.

Insight-Foraging Method 3. Relying on Knowledge and Intuition

This method relies on using the 1.6 zettabytes of data[13] inside your brain to identify information about the people you seek to serve:

- **Gut feeling.** Did you know that around 95 percent of our brain activity happens on autopilot?[14] We have knowledge (like the experiences we've lived through) that we simply cannot put into words because it's inaccessible to our conscious mind. This "gut feeling" is great for seasoned folks—years of knowledge help guide them. But newbies, be careful: if you haven't learned the ropes yet, don't trust your gut alone—it will leave you lost in the wilderness.

- **First principles.** These are the fundamental truths about how things work, including we humans. They're the bedrock of what we know to be *absolutely* true. Take, for instance, the way we think—a product of millions of years of evolution. That's a first principle. Throughout

---

12 To learn more about running interviews, I recommend *The Mom Test* by Rob Fitzpatrick (beginner level), *Talking to Humans* by Giff Constable (intermediate), and *The Jobs to Be Done Playbook* by Jim Kalbach (advanced).

13 Daniel Berger and Michał Januszewski. 2024. "Google AI: New Insights from 6 Images of the Human Brain." *The Keyword.* https://blog.google/technology/research/google-ai-research-new-images-human-brain/.

14 Daniel Kahneman. *Thinking, Fast and Slow.* Farrar, Straus and Giroux, 2011.

this book, I'll encourage you to view things through these funda-mental truths. Doing so will teach you to think for yourself in ways that most people don't.

- **Curiosity.** I don't think you can be creative without being curious about the world around you. The kind of curiosity that makes you forget you're blocking the entire charcuterie aisle at the supermarket because you're mesmerized by this guy desperately trying to sniff out the aroma of sliced pepperoni through the plastic packaging. The ability to observe without jumping to conclusions requires an open—and curious—mind.

Those are the three methods. Table 1.2 lets you compare all three.

Table 1.2. Comparing Insight-Foraging Methods

	Difficulty	Impact	Speed	Best for	Recommen-dation
Method 1. Looking at existing data	Moderate	Moderate	Varies	Access to internal data. Industries where reviews are common	Best when you have easy access to data
Method 2. Gathering new data	Difficult	High	Slow	In-depth insights when you don't have existing customers to rely on	Ideal for juicy insights without time pressure

	Difficulty	Impact	Speed	Best for	Recommendation
Method 3. Relying on knowledge and intuition	Easy	Limited	Fast	Quick overview. Getting a sense of the framework	Can use alone for a quick pass, or combine with other methods for depth

The Plan: Two Steps to Finding Juicy Insights

All right, fellow insight forager, it's time to get our hands dirty.

Step 1. Choose Your Focus

Foraging for insights requires *precision*. To avoid drowning in a sea of possibilities, you want to choose *one* specific area to gather insights on and make it stand the f*ck out. This is where you're going to direct your energy. Your focus area could be a specific product or service offering, a new client project, or an upcoming virtual event you're in charge of.

Please, please, please, don't skip this first step because *everything else* you need relies on this first decision. For a first run, I *strongly* recommend picking an area of focus that meets these criteria:

- **Direct control.** Choose something you have the power to influence and make decisions about so you can actually implement things—instead of producing more data that sits in drawers.

- **Emotional detachment.** Choose something you're not overly attached to to stay cool, calm, and collected, and keep your mind open to learning new things.

- **Manageable scope.** Start with something small enough to work through the framework efficiently so you can learn fast. Insight foraging can unearth a goldmine of information about your customers, and it's easy to feel overwhelmed. A smaller project lets you master the framework and control the flow of information before you tackle something more ambitious.

Table 1.3 gives my recommendations.

Table 1.3. Choosing the Right Area of Focus

Context	You could start with...	But don't begin with...
You're an experienced freelance marketer.	The most popular offering you're known for	Your entire business, including your podcast, newsletter, and social media profiles
You're a marketing agency owner.	A single client project you have a good relationship with or provide a specific service for	Repositioning your entire agency without your team involved
You're an individual contributor working for a fast-growing start-up.	Specific activities you're responsible for, such as an upcoming virtual event or an internal newsletter	Working on projects you don't "own" that involve a lot of red tape
You're the CEO of a boot-strapped start-up with a small marketing team.	Working with your marketing team to identify a specific market that needs your attention	Trying to overhaul the entire corporate strategy
You're a content creator with a growing audience.	A podcast you're thinking of starting	An entirely new business idea you thought about at lunch

Take a couple minutes to pick the specific area of focus that you will use throughout this first run.

TAKE ACTION

Picking one area to concentrate on lets you go deep. Instead of spreading yourself thin, you can use that energy to propel yourself through the rest of the framework. This laser focus prevents you from getting sidetracked.

Here's what to do:

- **Review Table 1.3.** Review the table and identify the scenario that best matches your current situation (freelancer, agency owner, etc.).

- **Choose wisely.** Based on your situation and the table's recommendations, select *one* specific area of focus for your **insight foraging**. This could be:

    ○ Your most popular service offering you want to make even more irresistible

    ○ A single client project you want to overdeliver on

    ○ An upcoming virtual event you want to get tons of sign-ups for

    ○ A specific market segment you want to attract

    ○ A new podcast idea you've been thinking about for the last two years

- **Keep it focused.** For a first round, ensure you have direct control over it, you're not too emotionally involved, and the workload is manageable.

- My area of focus is: _____

Step 2. Choose Your Path

All right, you've pinpointed your focus—*très bien!* Now let's map out how you'll gather those juicy insights. Think of it like a choose-your-own-adventure book where you pick the path that best suits your situation. Remember, there are three overall directions you can take to do so: looking at existing data (method 1), gathering new data (method 2), and, finally, using your knowledge and intuition (method 3).

Which path should you choose? To help decide, ask yourself these questions:

Do you have existing clients and access to them?

If **yes**, your path lies in extracting insights *directly* from your recent customers, whether it's data already available (method 1) like talking to sales, or extracting new info (method 2), like sending surveys or talking directly to your customers.

If you don't have an existing customer base or have no way to contact them, move on to the next question.

Do you have firsthand experience in the industry or category you're focusing on?

If **yes**, your path lies in extracting insights from customers of competitors and the industry as a whole (methods 1 and 2) and trusting your gut (method 3). It's more challenging than getting data from your own customers, but that's what makes it extremely valuable—if it were easy, everyone would do it.

If you don't know much about the sector you're planning on entering, there are more options below.

Is your industry an open book?

Can you easily find customer reviews or join online forums where customers congregate? For instance, online reviews are very common in the hospitality, e-commerce, and travel industries.

Yes? Then your path lies in extracting publicly available information from customers.

If **not**, this means you have *no easy way* to forage insights; the path to the forest is closed. If that's the case, it probably means you have to revisit your focus area from step 1.

Finally, how much time are you willing to invest in this process?

If you have **less than a day,** prioritize existing data and your own brain.

If you have **around a week,** you may be able to venture into collecting new insights.

If you have **more than a month,** for example, and you want to impress a new client, you have the luxury of gathering clean and juicy new data from sources other companies tend to gloss over. You can do so by, for example, interviewing customers and competitors' customers; by inviting your client's sales team to lunch so you can build rapport and learn more about what they know; or by becoming a secret shopper and spending a week or two observing how business is really done in your industry.

Figure 1.2 shows all the paths you can choose from.

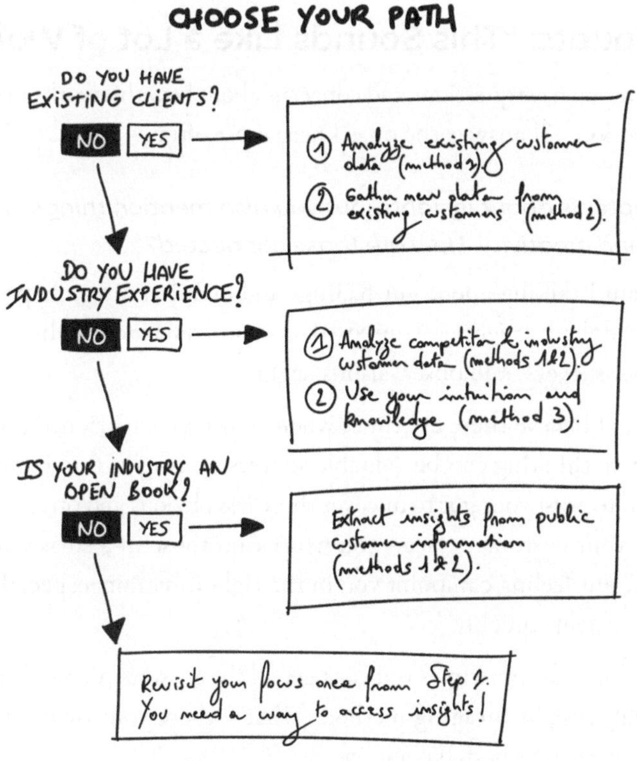

CHOOSE YOUR PATH

Figure 1.2. Choose-your-path flowchart.

TAKE ACTION

Take a few minutes to choose your path. Don't stress too much over the decision—you can always switch it up later, and chances are, you'll want to at some point.

My chosen path(s) for **insight foraging** is (are):

- _____
- _____
- _____

The Doubts: "This Sounds Like a Lot of Work!"

I'm sure you have questions and concerns about how this works in practice. In this section, I'll answer the ones I hear most often.

"This chapter is about insights, but you also mention things like gut feeling and creativity. How are those connected?"

Why am I talking about gut feelings and creativity in a chapter about insights? After all, insights are supposed to come from hard data like customer interviews, surveys, and observations, right?

Well . . . I believe there are times when your own experiences, intuition, and creative thinking can be valuable sources of insight, too. For example, you'll need to trust your gut to uncover those less obvious and often irrational struggles your customers face—you won't find those in a survey response. Also, your gut feeling can point you in the right direction, especially when you need insights quickly.

You'll find that sometimes you can't get all the answers you need just from "traditional" **insight-foraging** methods. That's where your own knowledge and experience (method 3) come in.

"How many clients do I need for reliable insights? How big should my dataset be?"

There is no *perfectly* accurate answer to this question; there's no magic number. But let me share with you a few guidelines to minimize the risks of unreliable insights:

1. **Start with triangulation.**[15] Aim for at least three different sources that back each other up. For example, if your survey, sales conversations, and review mining all tell a similar story, you're likely looking at information you can trust.

2. **Keep gathering data until you *stop* learning new information.** Experience helps here, but as a rule of thumb, keep going until you haven't unearthed any new insights.

3. **Navigate the tension between quality *and* quantity.** If you have loads of time, obsess over quantity with multiple sources, a larger pool of people, and statistically significant results. But if you're short on time, prioritize quality over quantity—you'll be surprised how much you can learn from *one* person with the right insights.

In short, balance data quantity with quality, triangulate your sources, and trust your gut to know when you've gathered enough insights.

"I don't want to bother my busy customers."

Once you tell the right customers you want to learn from them, they will want to be involved. Some will not answer or will say no and that's fine. You need to be comfortable with that.

"But didn't Steve Jobs say something like, 'F*ck the customers, I know best'?"

Nope. Not even close.

The Steve Jobs myth paints him as a lone wolf, a maverick who transformed Apple into the biggest brand in the world with sheer intuition. He's

---

15 This concept comes from Joanna Wiebe, founder of Copyhackers and the original conversion copywriter.

the guy who dared to defy convention, a visionary who could practically read minds. And since he supposedly never bothered with market research, why should you?

Here's the reality check: In 2011, Apple dragged Samsung to court, [16]claiming patent and copyright infringement. Apple won, but the legal battle unearthed something interesting—proof that Apple regularly used various forms of market research—tons and tons of it.

Sure, Jobs might have known better than to blindly ask customers what they wanted. But even Apple admits to "researching [its] installed base extensively" and "watching industry trends very carefully."[17]

Myth busted.

"People don't know what they want until you show it to them."

Exactly.

This is why it is critical to gather only insights from folks who have already invested resources in making progress. That's where the magic happens. And then it's your job to find the solution, not theirs.

The Recap: Creamy Mushroom Risotto

Just like a creamy mushroom risotto deserves quality ingredients, standing the f*ck out requires juicy customer insights. In this chapter, we learned to ditch the poisonous assumptions and unearth the raw, visceral truths about your customers.

Let's recap the key takeaways from this chapter:

- **Not all insights are created equal.** Focus on those who have recently invested time, money, or effort in solving the problem your business

---

16   Chris Martin. "Was Apple Founder Steve Jobs Right About Market Research?" *flexMR blog.* https://blog.flexmr.net/steve-jobs-market-research.

17   Jason Aten. 2021. "This Was Steve Jobs's Most Controversial Legacy. It Was Also His Most Brilliant." *Inc. Magazine.* https://www.inc.com/jason-aten/this-was-steve-jobs-most-controversial-legacy-it-was-also-his-most-brilliant.html.

addresses. Forget window shoppers and dormant customers—they're full of shit.

- **Three paths lead to juicy insights:**

  - **Existing data (method 1).** Mine reviews and internal conversations and talk to customer-facing staff.
  - **New data (method 2).** Observe customers in the wild, join their communities, have informal chats, run surveys, become a customer yourself, or conduct in-depth interviews.
  - **Knowledge and intuition (method 3).** Trust your gut (especially if you're seasoned), rely on first principles, and stay relentlessly curious.

- **Triangulate your sources.** Aim for at least three different sources that tell a similar story. This gives you confidence in your insights.

- **Don't be afraid to get your hands dirty.** The juiciest insights come from getting up close and personal with your customers' experiences.

- **Don't fall for the Steve Jobs myth.** Even Apple uses market research. Ditch the lone wolf myth and embrace the power of customer understanding.

2

The Juicy Insights

Meet César Alejandro Jaramillo (Figure 2.1), a former executive at a massive international consumer goods company with a goal: create an organic shampoo specifically for Latina women.

Figure 2.1. César Alejandro Jaramillo is one of the founders of LatinUs Beauty.

He and the other three founding members spent three years developing this shampoo for a segment of the population traditionally ignored by the beauty industry. Then they launched their online store, but there was a problem: they had plenty of website visitors through ads, yet most didn't buy. **César estimated their conversion rate was about 10 times lower than the industry standard.**

That's when he reached out to me for help after seeing me speak on a webinar. During our first call together, it became clear their low sales came from confusing messaging: **they had a really good product but never really explained** *why* **it stood the f*ck out and** *why* **Latina women should choose it over the competition.**

So we went **insight foraging.**

The LatinUs folks had two major strengths: **(1) they had recent customers** they could reach out to since they had launched online three months ago and **(2) they had** *decades* **of combined experience** in the beauty industry.

They had to increase sales and didn't have much time to figure this out. What do *you* think they should do next? Use existing data (method 1) like online reviews? Or maybe only use their knowledge (method 2) since they're all super experienced? Or maybe both?

What would *you* do in their situation?

The Problem: You Can't See the Label from Inside the Shampoo Bottle

Personally, I felt like they needed a jolt. **They had spent so much time in the lab developing their product and looking at consumer reports, they couldn't see the label from inside the shampoo bottle.**[18] In my opinion, they needed *fresh* insights from *real* people. Interviews with folks who bought from them recently (method 2) seemed like the right choice.

---

18 In *The Business of Expertise: How Entrepreneurial Experts Convert Insight to Impact + Wealth*, David C. Baker explains that "we can't read our own label from inside the jar." He highlights the difficulty of objectively assessing our own skills, knowledge, and position in the market.

Why? Because hearing similar stories from customers who do *not* know each other and using those stories to extract insights will help them get out of the shampoo bottle and get clarity.

The members of the team *personally* reached out to each of the customers who had bought from them over the last three months. The goal was simple—to understand how their very best customers were making decisions in order to infer:

- Which segment to start with

- Where to spend their limited resources

- What to say when people find them

- Why people should care

Figure 2.2 is a screenshot of an email César sent to a recent customer.

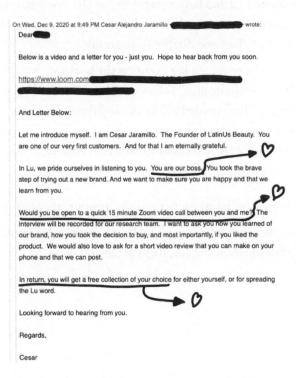

Figure 2.2. Email conversation between César (LatinUs cofounder) and a customer.

Notice the tone of the email? So kind and approachable. After just a few days of interviews, they were able to piece together a clear story, full of juicy insights:

LATINUS BEAUTY CUSTOMER STORY

Their best customers were **Latina women battling the relentless frizz of their long, thick hair.** Living in the **humid climate of Florida and California,** they were locked in a constant struggle against the elements. "When I go outside, I look like a witch!" (real quote)

LatinUs's customers were trapped in a **cycle of two-hour straightening marathons with rollers and blow dryers or weekly visits to their trusted Latino hairdresser** (no one else knew how to treat their hair). They'd shelled out cash for every shampoo under the sun, all with the same disappointing results.

And then the trigger: **a big event on the horizon.** A *quinceañera*, a night out with the girls, a chance to shine. Suddenly, the stakes were higher. They needed a solution, and they needed it *now*. This is where a **specialized shampoo,** one that promised to tame the frizz and make them feel more confident, entered the picture.

Adieu, overwhelming consumer reports. *Bonjour*, juicy customer story.

The team members started fresh to develop a message that stood the f*ck out and update their online ads, like the one in Figure 2.3.

Figure 2.3. One of LatinUs Beauty's best-performing ads.

Those changes tripled their revenue with the same ad budget. César sent me some proof a few weeks later—see Figure 2.4.

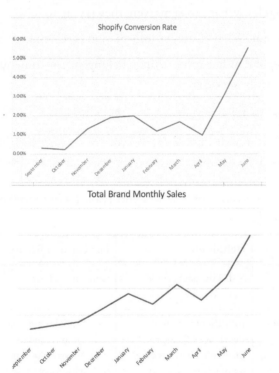

Figure 2.4. Conversion rate and total sales (per month).

This example shows how ditching generic customer data for real customer stories can make things clearer for everyone. This is the power of insight foraging and leveraging those six key insights: **job, alternative, struggle, segment, category,** and **trigger.** Everything else in the framework builds upon this foundation.

The Solution: Answer These Six Questions

I like to think of this process as understanding people's stories using six core questions:

1. **Job.** What did they try to accomplish?

2. **Alternatives.** What other solutions have they used or considered in the process?

3. **Struggles.** What problems were they trying to solve?

4. **Segment.** What customer information is relevant to the story?

5. **Category.** What other things belong in the same group as this product or service?

6. **Triggers.** What specific events compelled them to act?

Answering those six questions gives you the six juicy insights that act as the foundation of your quest to stand the f*ck out (see Table 2.1).

Table 2.1. The Six Types of Insights and Their Definition (Featuring LatinUs Beauty)

Insights	Definition	For LatinUs Beauty
1. Job	A specific goal people want to achieve	Control the frizz.
2. Alternatives	The different paths or solutions available to them, each with its own set of advantages and disadvantages	• Straightening their hair in a salon frequently • A two-hour hair care routine with rollers and blow dry • Trying all the shampoos from the supermarket

Insights	Definition	For LatinUs Beauty
3. Struggles	The obstacles and challenges that prevent them from making progress	"When I go outside, I look like a witch!" In other words, the warm, humid weather makes their long, frizzy hair go out of control.
4. Segment	The group of people with similar struggle(s) that we can serve in a way that gives us a distinct advantage against alternatives	Latinas with long, frizzy hair living in humid weather (mainly Florida and California)
5. Category	The group of things that solve similar struggle(s) in a similar way	Organic shampoo
6. Triggers	An event or a series of events that compel people to act	These customers had a big public event coming, like a birthday or a night out with the girls

Don't worry, I'll dig into each of those **insight** types throughout the next chapters. For now, I just want to make sure you understand the overall story you want to extract from **insight foraging,** outlined in Table 2.2.

Table 2.2. The Six Types of Insights and Their Definition (Featuring the PTDC)

Insights	Definition	For the PTDC
1. Job	A specific goal people want to achieve	Live a rich life.
2. Alternatives	The different paths or solutions available to them, each with its own set of advantages and disadvantages	• Knee-jerk reaction: do more of what they're already doing (more hours, more clients, more hustle). • Get half-naked on Instagram: give up their morals and worldview to attract more clients.

Insights	Definition	For the PTDC
3. Struggles	The obstacles and challenges that prevent them from making progress	• Lack of inner belief: they don't think they have a "real job," and neither do their friends and family. • Plenty of fitness knowledge, but not enough to run a real business
4. Segment	The group of people with similar struggle(s) that we can serve in a way that gives us a distinct advantage against alternatives	Jacked nerds: mature fitness trainers who enjoy being of service to others and want to truly impact the lives of others because they play the long game
5. Category	The group of things that solve similar struggle(s) in a similar way	Online fitness training
6. Triggers	An event or a series of events that compel people to act	• They get an online client out of the blue. A gym client moves to another city/country and wants to keep working with them. • A big change in their life: pregnancy, birthday, relationship, injury, free time, vacation, moving somewhere else • The final straw: a particularly bad day in a string of bad days (got fired, client quits, burned out, etc.)

Side Note:

In our framework, a **job** is a specific goal your customers want to achieve. This idea comes from the Jobs to Be Done (JTBD) theory: people "hire" products to fulfill needs in their lives. I've simplified JTBD for our practical use. Want to learn more? I recommend reading *The Jobs To Be Done* Playbook by Jim Kalbach.

The Plan: Start With Your Best Customers

Your quest to stand the f*ck out starts with one question: **What sparked the moment when recent customers knew they had to overcome a specific struggle or get a job done before even thinking about buying from you?**

Answering this question means uncovering how people make decisions. It's a pragmatic approach, using evidence of their past behavior to guide your next move. As underdogs, we can't afford to waste time on futurists or industry reports that try to predict the next 50 years. We need to be laser-focused on understanding what people are *already* doing and what's *already* working.

Step 1. Create a Central Place to Collect All Your Data

Think of it like your foraging basket—like the one in Figure 2.5—where you'd place the juiciest mushrooms. For every specimen you see, you'd come closer, take a quick look, and decide whether it's worth collecting.

Figure 2.5. That's what a foraging basket looks like in my head.

Please, **don't spend weeks building the prettiest, most functional basket ever.** In the woods, this doesn't matter. In other words, forget about fancy Notion templates with 78 tags, pretty colors, or advanced automation.

All you really need is a big table with one column per customer and six rows for the six types of insights we want to collect, as shown in Table

2.3. You can use a spreadsheet, pen and paper, or clay tablets. Just keep it super simple.

Table 2.3. Insight-Foraging Template

	Individual /Source A	Individual /Source B	Individual /Source C	...	Individual /Source X
1. Job					
2. Alternatives					
3. Struggles					
4. Segment					
5. Category					
6. Triggers					

TAKE ACTION

Before you start gathering insights, you need a central place to store and organize your findings. You don't need fancy software or elaborate systems—even if bigger competitors use them.

Create a table based on the template in Table 2.3, with one row per customer and six columns representing the six types of insights you'll be collecting: **job, alternatives, struggles, segment, category,** and **triggers.**

Step 2. Start With Your Best Customers

You're standing at the edge of the forest, but in which direction should you even go? For example, porcini mushrooms tend to prefer established forests with loads of shade, and they tend to thrive on slopes/hillsides. If it's your first time mushrooming, this is where you'd start.

Well, it's the same when foraging insights. **To find the juiciest ones, start with your *best* customers.** I'm being intentionally vague here because I'm *not* asking you to pick your niche, or target audience, or whatever else you want to call it (we'll cover that later in Stage 2, "Unique Positioning").

Instead, try to think about the people you enjoy working with the most— they just get it and don't drain your soul. Or if it's not your business, ask the people in charge who they think are their best customers. If you don't have any customers yet, use your intuition. Or ask people who have bought a similar product, or have done something to reach their goal.

How does this step align with focusing on *recent* customers to avoid poisonous insights? Your "best" customers are probably those you've built relationships with over time, not necessarily the newest additions who've bought from you very recently. **My recommendation?** *Combine* **the two. Focus your energy on recent customers who** *resemble* **your best ones.** It's like channeling your focus on those best customers to naturally filter out the recent ones who don't match that vibe.

When I do this exercise with clients, I ask them to tell me *everything* **they can about each person whom they consider to be a great customer. I want to hear their story;** who they are, why they like them, how they met, and so on . . . I'm not interested in the traditional demographic information like their age, their job title, or the name of their last pet.

TAKE ACTION

Who are the people you love working with? That's who we're digging into right now. Not to define your niche but to uncover the juicy insights that make them tick. D'accord?

Here's the plan:

1. **Who's your fave?** If you work with clients, whom do you love working with? If not, whom does your company value most? No customers yet? Maybe you are your best customer.

2. **Write a vivid description of these people.** Forget age, job title, and so on, for now. Who are they? Why do you like them?

My best customers: _____

_____

_____

The Doubts: "Is This Process Really Needed?"

"I know my industry and what customers want. No need to do any research."

Do you, really?

Marketing professor Mark Ritson said it best on my podcast: "The minute you start getting paid, it's impossible to see that product the way your customers see it. You are not the customer. Turn the lights on. Make everyone appreciate that we're standing in the dark."[19]

There's no downside to foraging insights, especially when you know which insights to pay attention to and which to ignore.

19   Mark Ritson. 2018. "4 Steps to Creating a Rock-Solid Marketing Strategy." *Everyone Hates Marketers*. https://www.everyonehatesmarketers.com/podcast/63-mark-ritson-marketing-week.

"I don't really like my current customers. What should I do? What if I want to attract a different type of customer?"

This could be a sign that you need to take a step back to understand why. Is it just that you don't like them right now because you're mentally exhausted? Or is it that you have never liked them? If it's the latter and you're a business owner, going through the methodology with another business idea might be more productive.

"This process really scares me."

I understand. Truly, I do. But going through this process is what it takes to stand the f*ck out in a noisy world. You should really be scared of one thing and one thing only: *obscurity.*[20]

The Recap: Understand Customers' Stories

Remember César, his cofounders, and their shampoo for Latina women? They had a great product but struggled to sell it because they were stuck inside the shampoo bottle, relying on assumptions instead of real customer insights. Standing the f*ck out starts with ditching the guesswork and unearthing the raw, visceral truths about your customers. This chapter is about understanding their stories, not predicting the future.

Let's recap the key takeaways from this chapter:

- There are six core insights to uncover:

  1. **Job.** What did they try to accomplish?

  2. **Alternatives.** What other solutions have they used or considered in the process?

  3. **Struggles.** What problems were they trying to solve?

  4. **Segment.** What customer information is relevant to the story?

---

20 In my first interview with Seth Godin, he said, "What we want in a low-trust world is someone to trust. Our problem is not piracy; our problem is obscurity." 2017. "Seth Godin's Marketing Secrets to Launching a New Business." *Everyone Hates Marketers.* https://podcast.everyonehates-marketers.com/episodes/seth-godins-marketing-secrets-to-launching-a-new-business.

5. **Category.** What other things belong in the same group as this product or service?

6. **Triggers.** What specific events compelled them to act?

- *Oui,* **you can ditch the fancy tools.** A basic table with columns for each of the six insights and rows for each customer is all you need.

- **Start with your best recent customers.** Identify recent customers who look like your ideal clients. Their fresh perspectives hold the juiciest insights.

- **Forget about demographics.** Focus on vivid, personal stories instead of traditional demographics.

- **You are not your customer.** Get out of your own head and into theirs.

3

The Patterns

If you're into mushrooming, you'll know that you can buy field guides to help you identify wild mushrooms.

Knowing your mushrooms is rather important if you want to, you know, *live*. Porcini mushrooms blend right in with dead leaves, all brown and round and innocent-looking. But get this—there's a look-alike, the Devil's bolete, that could really ruin your day. And by ruin, I mean . . . well, let's just say you don't want to find out the hard way.

Do you know what field guides are useless at, though? Giving you *exact* spots to find mushrooms. That's because mushrooms sprout semi-randomly based on factors you can't control, such as temperature, moisture, and nutrient availability. This makes it impossible to predict *where* and *when* they will appear.

The Problem: There's No Map . . .

Growth hacks. Quick fixes. Instant results. Simple tweaks.

We're inundated with advice promising us that selling stuff to people is easy. "Just follow those 14 steps!" they say. And then, when we can't seem to make it work, we doubt ourselves.

With marketing, just like mushrooming, there's no fucking map. You have to experience things yourself. You have to get out and wander through the forest without a GPS. You have to seek discomfort.

The Solution: . . but There Are Guidelines

So, look. Don't expect a treasure map with a big, fat X marking the spot where all the juicy insights are buried. That part is up to *you*. Anyone trying to sell you that kind of shortcut is full of *merde*.

Here's what I can offer you instead . . . a set of guidelines to give you the best chance to unearth juicy insights:

1. **Do not expect to find all six insights every time you talk to a customer or read an online review.** Sometimes nothing interesting will come up, while other times, you might strike gold by getting the full story from one source.

2. **You want to be open and curious about your customer's thought process from start to finish.** Yes, you might miss some details occasionally, but this is how you learn and gather insights. Think of yourself as an adventurer, here to explore.

3. **Every time you come across an insight, record it with care.** Once again, this could be the piece of information that could be used as the core of standing the f*ck out against top dogs. Specifically, record what you hear, see, or read *without* summarizing it.

4. **Add depth by noting the emotions you can sense.** Are customers using negative, emotionally charged language to describe their anger, fear, or even disgust? Or are they using positive language? Also, depending on the method you use, pay attention to nonverbal cues like facial expressions or body language.

5. **Only pay attention to insights coming from people who have recently invested resources—such as time, money, and/or effort—to address the problem you're interested in solving.** *Oui, oui*, it bears repeating. If you have any doubt or sense something's wrong, always trust your judgment.

6. **Don't let others pick insights on your behalf (if possible).** It could be tempting to outsource this entire process to a human (or a machine) to save time. But I must caution you against it. Of course, you don't have to do all the groundwork yourself, but you do need to take part in the journey one way or another to make sure you don't miss subtle details that could give you an edge.

Now that you have the overall guidelines to guide you, Table 3.1 shows how to spot specific insights.

Table 3.1. Field Guide Summary

Insights	Questions	What to Look For	Example
1. Job	What did they try to accomplish?	Objectives and expected results	"[I want] long, beautiful hair that everyone can see."
2. Alternatives	What other solutions have they used or considered in the process?	The work-arounds, hacks, and other solutions they have considered or used to reach their goal	"I considered hiring interns to do the work instead of using software."
3. Struggles	What problems were they trying to solve?	Extreme emotions— such as frustration, anger, or joy—about what they dreaded doing or annoyed them	"I'm sick of being late for picking up the kiddos from daycare again."
4. Segment	What customer information is relevant to the story?	What they say about themselves, such as worldviews, beliefs, or interests. What you've observed about them	"I've been in the fitness industry since the late 80s and I've seen it all."

Insights	Questions	What to Look For	Example
5. Category	What other things belong in the same group as this product or service?	How people describe what is offered in their own words	"Oh . . . so it's like normal paint, but washable?"
6. Triggers	What specific events compelled them to act?	Precise moments in time led them closer to making a decision Context: When did it happen? Where? With whom? With what?	"My boss said we couldn't have phones at work anymore, so I bought a smartwatch."

Here are my recommendations for the most common **insight-foraging** methods. This should be more than enough for you to feel confident exploring the woods in search of juicy insights.

Insight Foraging with . . . Customer Interviews

With customer interviews, you get to ask questions in a controlled environment to uncover insights. This works well with recent, complex purchases where a lot was at stake and many people were involved—which is why it's a popular choice for folks selling to B2B companies. In other words, do *not* use interviews for folks who bought something quickly without thinking too much about it—like the Crayola washable paint bottles I bought 12 days ago.

Although this is called a customer *interview*, do not treat the exercise as one. You're simply conversing casually with someone you want to learn more about. Keep the six insights in mind, but don't obsess over trying to get precise answers for every question.

I like to start the conversation with something to the effect of: "Bonjour, bonjour [first name], thanks so much for taking the time to talk to me; it means a lot. Again, I'm not trying to sell you anything. I'm working on [area of focus], and I want to learn as much from you as possible so we can stand the f*ck out."

Then I get into small talk to build rapport. I ask things like, "Where are you based? What's the weather like where you are? What's that painting behind you? What's that microphone you're using?"

Then depending on where you are, you may want to ask permission to record: "Is it OK to record this conversation? It's for internal purposes only and it allows me to listen to you instead of taking too many notes."

Then I like to start the "real" interview without mentioning it. I just get started with small and easy questions to build people's confidence before getting to more complex ones: "In which department do you work? How long have you been working there? Is French the sexiest accent?"

This is when I like to dig deep to understand the story—*their* story: "OK, let's go back in time a bit. Do you remember the first time you thought about [getting the **job** done, solving this **struggle**]? Yes? OK, tell me more."

I never trust their first answer and always aim to go deeper: "Oh yes? What do you mean? How did you go about it? OK, that sounds super interesting. Tell me more, puh-lease." Focus on the past (not the future).

I end the call by asking if this conversation sparked any comments, questions, thoughts—anything at all. Sometimes this last prompt delivers the juiciest insights, so give people time to think about it before wrapping up.

Insight Foraging with . . . Surveys

With surveys, you can ask questions in an asynchronous way. This works best if you have many existing customers that you can easily contact via email. You can then follow up with some of the respondents for a proper interview to dig deeper.

I like to test my questions before sending a questionnaire to a large number of people. There's a certain art to creating prompts that elicit good answers and it's unlikely you will get it right the first time around.

When testing, I like to look for telltale signs that my questions need to be improved:

- Responses like "Huh?" or "I don't know"

- Answers that *completely* miss the point of the question
- Nonanswers or vague replies
- Formatting issues that confuse respondents (like using single-line input for questions that require longer responses)

You'd be surprised how differently people can interpret your words. By refining your questions based on these test responses, you'll increase your chances of uncovering valuable **insights** when you send out the final questionnaire.

Just like with interviews, you want to start with small and easy questions to build their confidence. Multiple-choice questions are helpful here so respondents can *"warm up."*

Also, as a rule of thumb, treat *one* question as *one* thing you want to know—don't bundle a bunch of questions together because it's very overwhelming for participants. For example, "What other solutions did you consider, and what's the one thing you love about our product?" is a multilayered question that should be split into two.

Use open-ended questions to uncover the insights you're really interested in unearthing. Instead of asking about hypothetical situations or settling for a simple yes or no, encourage people to open up and share their experiences. For example, instead of asking, "Did you consider other shampoos before buying this one?," try something like, "What other solutions did you explore when looking for a shampoo?" See the difference? Open-ended questions like this invite detailed responses and uncover the "why" behind people's actions.

As a final tip, I always end my surveys with something like, "Is there anything else you'd like to add? Don't be shy! We love feedback." Just like with interviews, this sometimes leads to some golden nuggets.

Insight Foraging with . . . Reviews

With review mining, you want to find places where people have shared their recent experiences about specific products or services. It's my personal favorite when I'm strapped for time and want to get a head start.

My best tip is to pay attention *only* to long, passionate reviews that describe an experience either *very* positively or *very* negatively. You probably have limited time to get this done, so please save your brainpower for the most interesting reviews.

Use your gut to weed out reviews that sound fake or clearly written to get something in return. For example, if a review sounds too good to be true, too polished, or way too enthusiastic about what it's describing, it probably is.

Insight Foraging with . . . Communities

This technique relies on participating in online communities, forums, or virtual conferences where your segment already congregates to observe what's being said. Sometimes being a member of just one of those communities can be more than enough to find juicy insights.

In a similar way to review mining, you want to focus your attention on posts with loads of engagement (such as number of comments) and highly emotional content. And then, of course, look for evidence of past behavior—not hypothetical future actions—to make sure your foraging basket does not contain poisonous specimens.

Insight Foraging with . . . the Fly-on-the-Wall Technique

This is Mark Ritson's favorite technique for making his clients—senior marketers working for huge brands—realize they're "standing in the dark." He would take them out into the field and get them to hang out with customers while their products were being chosen and consumed. Obviously, this works particularly well in retail, where you can just go to a shop and observe people in their natural habitat.

This is a bit challenging in more secretive environments, but still doable. Nothing stops you from contacting B2B clients, for example, and asking them if you could be a fly on the wall for one day to observe how they get things done. Sure, you won't map out their entire sales cycle, but you might develop your empathy and curiosity. Who knows what unexpected gems you'll uncover?

Insight Foraging with . . . Method Marketing

With method marketing, you don't just *think* about your customers; you *become* them. You want to try to experience what they experience, see the world through their eyes, and use the products they use.

Think of Robert De Niro in *Taxi Driver*. To accurately portray Travis Bickle, he immersed himself in the character's world, even driving a taxi every weekend.[21] The result was a raw and authentic performance.

This technique is especially useful if you're new to an industry since it helps you understand your customers by putting yourself in their shoes. It's not perfect. You *won't* be experiencing the product or service for real since you're *pretending*, but that doesn't mean it's useless.

Here's my advice: record *every single thought* you have, especially at the start. Don't dismiss anything as irrelevant. The beauty lies in capturing those raw, first-time impressions that you can get only once.

This is a very accessible technique, with one caveat: If you're already an expert in your sector, you might know *too much*. You won't be able to see things from a beginner's eyes, which, in turn, means that you may be unable to extract juicy insights.

The Plan: Look for Patterns in Data

Step 1. Put All the Data You Collect in the Same Place

Your goal is to go through all the data you've gathered and soak it in. Since insight foraging is mentally demanding, focus all your attention on it. My advice? Find a quiet place, silence your phone, eliminate *any* distractions, and aim for one- to two-hour sessions so your brain doesn't fry too quickly.

Start by gathering all your data in one place. Then prioritize the most compelling pieces—the ones that resonate with you and align with your ideal customer. Think about the reviews that jumped out at you, the inter-

21 Aimee Ferrier. 2023. "The Wild Method Acting Stories of Robert De Niro." *Far Out Magazine*. https://faroutmagazine.co.uk/wild-method-acting- stories-of-robert-de-niro/.

views that sparked your curiosity, and the customer interactions that left a lasting impression.

Step 2. Extract Key Moments

This step is all about understanding customers as *individuals* first, *before* finding patterns. To do it, use the Insight-Foraging template in Table 3.2. Each row represents one specific insight type, and each column represents one individual or source.

Table 3.2. Insight-Foraging Template

	Individual /Source A	Individual /Source B	Individual /Source C	. . .	Individual /Source X
1. Job					
2. Alternatives					
3. Struggles					
4. Segment					
5. Category					
6. Triggers					

When I come across some potentially useful data like an interview transcript or a long review, I like to start by reading it once to get an idea of what I might be able to find. After the first reading, I read it a second time and start extracting key moments that look like they could fit into one of the six types of **insight** I'm looking for.

Do your best to capture detailed information with plenty of context. If a piece of information fits multiple categories, include it in both. The goal is *clarity*, not brevity.

Example:

Tania Stacey, cofounder of East Forged (an Australian cold brew tea company), found a clever way to gather insights after Covid. By setting up shop at massive makers markets—three-day events with over 10,000 attendees—Tania (seen in Figure 3.1) and her team were able to interact with thousands of potential customers and uncover super-juicy insights.

Figure 3.1. Tania Stacey talking to a customer sampling the company's products.

The team members at East Forged made a point of documenting their experiences at these markets. Over 36 markets, 26,000 tastings, 5,000 customer interactions, and they took notes on everything they observed. It wasn't foolproof, as they had to rely on their memories if they were super busy pouring samples of their tea. However, they would always write up notes at the end of each day. Tania was generous enough to share with me their field notes from one of the markets. Table 3.3 captures what stood out to me.

Table 3.3. Insight-Foraging Field Notes from East Forged

	Questions	Sidney Market—Field Notes
1. Job	What did people try to accomplish?	[Nothing relevant came up.]
2. Alternatives	What other solutions have they used or considered in the process?	[Nothing relevant came up.]

	Questions	Sidney Market—Field Notes
3. Struggles	What problems were they trying to solve?	Two people said they were avoiding tea because they didn't want to stain their teeth.
4. Segment	What customer information is relevant to the story?	15 can cartons sold today. A dad shopping with wife and two daughters. Their whole family liked the green tea. Other sales of cartons came from young couples. Lots of couples buying together or groups of friends mixing up their favorites in a four-pack
5. Category	What other things belong in the same group as this product or service?	The white tea has been a standout. We did sell out on Sunday.
6. Triggers	What specific events compelled them to act?	A good number (at least 20 to 30) people have bought us before and brought their friends. I find they always love to share. Lots of people asked, "When would I drink this?" I started saying it's great as an afternoon pick-me-up and a wonderful accompaniment to food. People responded, "Oh, I can see it working with fatty/heavy foods or really delicate foods." Occasion mattered, as otherwise healthy hydration was what everyone else was doing.

I wanted to share this with you to show that you don't need perfectly clean, precise data to extract insights. If I only had one hour to spare to forage for insights and infer a few themes, this would be more than enough to go through each stage of the methodology.

Example:

Let's go back to our friends selling shampoo for Latinas. Table 3.4 presents the main points from customer interviews the founders conducted when we worked together.

Table 3.4: Insight-Foraging Interviews for LatinUs Beauty

Insights	Questions	Rain/35-Year-Old	Luisa/55-Year-Old
1. Job	What did they try to accomplish?	"My hair stays straight for two days. I was so impressed"	"[I want] long beautiful hair that everyone can see."
2. Alternatives	What other solutions have they used or considered in the process?	"I usually go and smell the shampoos. I want now to smell like your shampoo; I don't even use perfume any more." "It is thick, not runny or watery like other shampoos."	"I am waiting for a miracle. I would love to have bouncy curls, but as it is not possible, I spend two hours straightening them to make them look beautiful." "I've tried all the shampoos that seem natural and what hairdressers recommend." "I only go to Latino hairdressers. Americans don't know how to deal with Latin hair. I do think it is different."
3. Struggles	What problems were they trying to solve?	"I have dandruff, and I need to wash almost every day." "It is either stress making it fall out or a bad shampoo."	"I was bullied for ugly hair. Mom did not take the time to fix it and chopped it. Now I want long hair, and it takes two hours."

Insights	Questions	Rain/35-Year-Old	Luisa/55-Year-Old
4. Segment	What customer information is relevant to the story?	"My hair is like a mood." "I am learning Spanish through telenovelas."	
5. Category	What other things belong in the same group as this product or service?		"American hair is flat and Afro-American hair is curly. We are in between, so we need a special shampoo. There is nothing like it today in the market."
6. Triggers	What specific events compelled them to act?	Saw Victoria Ruffo* unboxing on Instagram	

A Mexican actress notable for her roles in telenovelas.

Example:

And finally, I want to show you how fast you can extract insights from information freely available online. I went to Amazon, searched for Jon Goodman's books, picked the one with the most reviews—*Ignite the Fire*—and selected one customer review that looked genuinely interesting. Figure 3.1 shows the insights that jumped out at me.

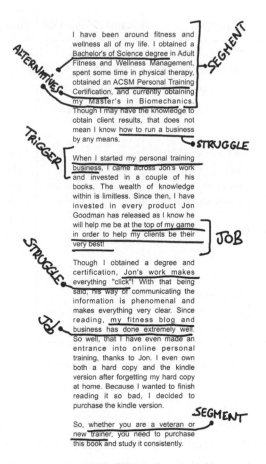

Figure 3.2. My analysis of the insights provided by a reader of Coach Goodman's book, Ignite the Fire.

Table 3.5 shows the same analysis with the main insights I found, sorted by each type of insight.

Table 3.5. Insight-Foraging Reviews for the PTDC

	Questions	Joshua//Amazon Review
1. Job	What did people try to accomplish?	"Be at the top of my game in order to help my clients be their very best!" "My fitness blog and business have done extremely well."

	Questions	Joshua//Amazon Review
2. Alternatives	What other solutions have they used or considered in the process?	Bachelor's of Science degree ACSM Personal Training Certification Master's in Biomechanics
3. Struggles	What problems were they trying to solve?	"How to run a business" "Jon makes everything 'click'!"*
4. Segment	What customer information is relevant to the story?	"I've been around fitness and wellness all of my life." Degree + Certification
5. Category	What other things belong in the same group as this product or service?	[Nothing relevant came up.]
6. Triggers	What specific events compelled them to act?	"When I started my personal training business"

Reading between the lines, it seems like this reviewer had trouble connecting the dots between his knowledge of fitness and the "real world" of business. It's not explicitly said, but that's what I understood from it.

At this stage, just focus on capturing the key moments and *loosely* assigning them to any relevant insight categories. Don't get bogged down in making everything perfectly aligned. We'll refine these connections and make them more precise later.

When extracting key moments:

1. Focus on one source at a time.

2. Read the source twice.

3. Label observations using the six insight types.

4. Provide ample context for each insight.

5. Don't worry about perfect categorization at this stage.

TAKE ACTION

It's time to uncover juicy insights within your data. Here's what to do:

1. **Gather your data.** This could be interview transcripts, customer reviews, survey responses—anything that captures your customer's voice.

2. **Skim for context.** Quickly read through what you've collected to get a feel for the overall story it tells.

3. **Extract key moments.** As you read a second time, pinpoint specific phrases or sentences that relate to the six types of insight: job, alternatives, struggles, segment, category, and triggers. Don't worry about perfect categorization yet; just capture anything interesting.

4. **Organize your findings.** Use a table like the previous examples. And remember, even seemingly insignificant details can spark powerful insights later on.

Step 3. Look for Patterns

For each type of insight, start looking for possible patterns. What seems to be coming up over and over again? Sometimes it's super easy—almost like the data is screaming at you. Other times it could feel like there are no common themes whatsoever.

To do this, for each key moment you found in the previous step, look for (1) what the moments have in common and (2) how they differ. Key moments that are similar to each other can become a theme. And then themes that are completely different from each other must be separate. Use the template in Table 3.6 to identify the themes.

Table 3.6. Pattern Template

	Theme A	Theme B	...	Theme X
1. Job				
2. Alternatives				
3. Struggles				
4. Segment				
5. Category				
6. Triggers				

When faced with a large amount of data, it's normal to feel overwhelmed. Don't panic if patterns aren't immediately apparent. You aren't going to get flashing lights saying, *This is the insight!* In other words, you're not looking for a single major insight but rather differences and small details that could be significant.

Example:

Going back to East Forged, the Australian cold brew tea company. I've looked at their field notes and combined them with customer reviews I found online to identify patterns. There were themes that jumped out at me, particularly for the **alternatives**: most customers mentioned they used cold brew tea as a substitute for alcoholic beverages. This is an example of an insight that's screaming at you. (See Table 3.7.)

Table 3.7. East Forged Alternatives

	Questions	Theme A
2. Alternatives	What other solutions have they used or considered in the process?	Alcohol, in particular beer

I also found obvious patterns when it came to the job customers were "hiring" this drink to do around the ideas of (1) treating themselves and (2) refreshment. As for the way the cold brew drinkers were describing it (besides just cold brew tea), the two themes that came up were (1) nonalcoholic alternative and (2) unsweetened/zero-calorie drink. (See Table 3.8.)

Table 3.8. East Forged Job and Category

	Questions	Theme A	Theme B	Theme C
1. Job	What did they try to accomplish?	Treat myself, relax, and enjoy.	Refreshing	
5. Category	What other things belong in the same group as this product or service?	Cold brew tea	Nonalcoholic alternative	Unsweetened, zero calories

It's when examining **struggles** and **segment** information that I've felt I've found super-juicy insights. First, the idea that it's appealing to folks who can't/don't drink alcohol (like during pregnancy) and those who can't/don't consume too much sugar (e.g., folks with diabetes). Second, I really like the idea that this cold brew tea is seen as a fancy "adult" treat. It implies that people want *more* than just a refreshing drink that tastes great: they care about the way it looks and feels to them (and others). (See Table 3.9.)

Table 3.9. East Forged Struggles and Segment

	Questions	Theme A	Theme B	Theme C	Theme D	Theme E
3. Struggles	What problems were they trying to solve?	Low/zero calories	Great taste, mouth feel	Fancy, adult treat	Teeth stain	

	Ques-tions	Theme A	Theme B	Theme C	Theme D	Theme E
4. Segment	What customer information is relevant to the story?	Sobriety	Pregnancy	Diabetes	Family with kids	Young couples

And finally, I've found a lot of interesting specific situations—**triggers**—associated with this drink. Some may sound obvious, like when the weather is super hot, but others, like at the beginning of the weekend or during special times of the year, further connect with the fancy "adult" treat idea. (See Table 3.10.)

Table 3.10. East Forged Triggers

	Questions	Theme A	Theme B	Theme C	Theme D
6. Triggers	What specific events compelled them to act?	At the end of the day	When the wea-ther is hot (summer)	After sports activities	During spe-cial times of the year (Chris-tmas)
		Theme E	**Theme F**	**Theme G**	
		Discovered during market	At the beginning of the week-end (Friday night, night out with frie-nds)	With fatty or really delicate food	

You've probably noticed, but it bears repeating: This is a subjective exercise, of course, and that's by design. Why? By trusting your ability to spot unique connections that others might miss, you are already developing a distinct advantage that may help you stand the f*ck out.

For example, while looking for patterns, I zeroed in on this fancy "adult" treat concept because it gave me plenty of ideas for the next steps. But you may have paid more attention to another insight, and that's OK, too!

To sum up this step, my advice is to:

- Label your themes without losing the essence of what customers are saying.

- Don't stress if themes aren't exactly identical—just merge them if they're similar enough.

- You might have 5 to 6 themes per insight type, totaling around 30 to 40 themes overall. Prioritize patterns that appear frequently (in 80 percent of responses) while remaining open to smaller groups that stick out.

The goal is to create a clear picture of your audience's journey without getting bogged down in perfectionism.

TAKE ACTION

You have a mountain of insights. Now dig for gold. Here's how:

1. **Comb through your insights.** For each element (job, alternatives, struggles, etc.), look for similarities and add them to your pattern template.

2. **Group them.** If you see a theme, write it down under the matching element in your table.

3. **Trust your gut.** If a pattern feels important, it probably is. Your unique perspective is your superpower.

Step 4. And Then . . . Stop

You will never, ever, *ever* have perfect data. You will always feel like you are missing something. You will most likely feel the urge to get one more survey answer, one more customer interview, one more conversation with sales . . . But just like when hunting for mushrooms on a warm, sunny day, you eventually have to come home.

1. **Set a firm deadline:** *By that [specific date], I will move on to Stage 2 of the Stand The F*ck Out methodology.*

2. **Fucking commit to it.**

Remember, I've built this framework to adapt to your specific needs, and you can go through it as many times as you want. This means you can start with a handful of data, go through the next three stages, see how it feels, and then do it again with a bit more data, go through the other three stages . . . You get it.

This approach will make you happier and more confident. You want to settle for good enough when it fits your standards instead of spending weeks or months—or even years!—agonizing over decisions like the "big guys." This is once again how you can win as an underdog.

TAKE ACTION

My **insight-foraging** deadline is: __ /__ /____. Then I commit to moving on to the next stage.

The Doubts: "What if I Can't Find Insights or People to Talk To?"

"What if I can't find any juicy insights?"

You may have good insight, but you don't trust it right away. Or you think it's too obvious and there must be something better. I've been doing this **insight foraging** for a while now, and my simple tip for you is to give yourself time to digest it all. You're probably too close to the data and the business to see the insights for what they are.

"How do I know if I've found an insight or not?"

You'll know you've likely found an insight when you uncover something that surprises you, contradicts your assumptions, or makes you laugh. Juicy insights often make you pause and add a layer of understanding that explains why people do what they do.

Key signs of an insight include:

- Surprising information that challenges your existing beliefs
- Recurring **struggles** you hadn't previously identified
- Explanations for customer behavior that suddenly make things click

"Where can I find people to talk to?"

This is the ultimate pressure test. How can you find clients to pay for your stuff if you can't find customers to talk to? This is not meant to be a dig—it's meant to highlight how **insight foraging** is closely linked to making sales.

Say you're in a situation where you do not have an existing customer base to survey and/or talk to directly. And say that reviews are not available either. You want to find customers who've recently bought from a direct or indirect competitor or from the sector in which you operate.

Think gathering insights from competitors is impossible? Think again.

Director of product marketing Sarah MacKinnon got on a call with four customers of a big competitor. This is a big deal, given how precious insights like this are. She looked at the competitor's website and case studies. Her goal was to identify companies doing business with this competitor. Then she went on LinkedIn to find folks working inside those companies. And finally she sent them a note to connect, like the one in Figure 3.2.

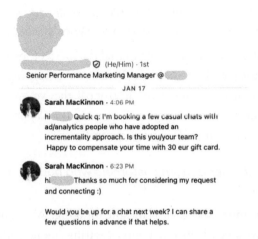

(He/Him) · 1st
Senior Performance Marketing Manager @

JAN 17

Sarah MacKinnon · 4:06 PM
hi   Quick q: I'm booking a few casual chats with
ad/analytics people who have adopted an
incrementality approach. Is this you/your team?
Happy to compensate your time with 30 eur gift card.

Sarah MacKinnon · 6:23 PM
hi   Thanks so much for considering my request
and connecting :)

Would you be up for a chat next week? I can share a
few questions in advance if that helps.

Figure 3.3. Example of a LinkedIn message sent by Sarah to a competitor's client

Out of about 50 messages, Sarah got to chat with four people—which is, it bears repeating, a big deal! She used what she learned to put together a buyer journey that she and the sales team could get behind in order to put together a plan to attract customers.

There are no shortcuts here. This takes real work, but it'll be all worth it once you come across game-changing insights:

- **Ask for introductions from the people in your network.** Do they know anyone they could introduce you to?

- **Find testimonials/case studies on competitors' websites and reach out to the people who were contributing.** Yes, yes, this is cheeky—but you're not trying to sell anything, remember?

- **Post in the online communities you're a part of.** You never know; you might stumble upon someone who's in a good mood.

- **Send cupcakes through the mail.** This is semi-serious advice. That's what I did in the early days of my first marketing agency. I'd find the address of the offices where the people I wanted to talk to worked, and then find a bakery nearby and ask the bakery folks to deliver cupcakes.

"It's difficult to know whether people have already invested resources and will be worth talking to. What should I do?"

Instead of getting stuck trying to find the "perfect" people (who may not even exist!), use your best judgment. When you're reaching out for customer interviews or surveys, simply ask up front if they've invested resources in finding a solution. If someone doesn't pan out the way you hoped, just hold onto the insights that truly matter and move on.

"Is it sufficient to learn from customers who bought a similar thing before?"

Oui. Remember the goal of **insight foraging.** We want to learn from folks who have recently invested resources (time, money, effort) into solving similar problems to yours. They don't have to have bought the exact same thing. For example, if you were selling shampoo for Latinas, you could find people who straighten their hair in a salon frequently or those who spend hours every week trying to tame it with rollers and blow drying.

The Recap: Ditch the Treasure Map

There's no magic map when looking for insights, but there are guidelines to help you navigate the wilderness. This chapter gave you the approach you need to become really good at discovering juicy customer information.

Let's recap the key takeaways:

- **Embrace the chaos.** You won't always uncover every insight, and that's perfectly fine. Focus on gathering rich, contextual information from recent customers.

- **The most common insight-foraging methods are:**

    ◦ **Customer interviews.** Ask questions in a controlled environment.
    ◦ **Surveys.** Ask questions in an asynchronous way.
    ◦ **Review mining.** Mine places where people have shared their experiences.
    ◦ **Communities.** Participate in online communities, forums, or virtual conferences where your segment already congregates.

- ◦ **The fly-on-the-wall technique.** Hang out with customers while their products are being chosen and consumed.
  - ◦ **Method marketing.** Don't just think about your customers; become them.

- **Look for patterns, prioritize, and then STOP.** Don't get lost in the weeds. Set a firm deadline for your insight foraging, identify recurring themes, and move on to Stage 2.

- **No customers?** *Pas de problème!* Get scrappy and reach out to your network, competitor's clients, or online communities. Remember those cupcakes!

The Recap: Insight Foraging

Insight foraging is the first stage in the Stand The F*ck Out framework. It's about ditching assumptions we all have about our market. Instead, we collected juicy insights that are going to be the very foundation of your quest to standing the f*ck out.

Let's recap the key takeaways from this stage:

- **Focus on recent customers who've invested resources.** Ignore anyone else. Focus on those who recently bought a product or invested time in solving a problem similar to yours. They provide the juiciest insights.

- **Let go of the demographics; embrace the stories.** *Let it goooo, let it goooooooooooooooo!* Forget age, job title, the name of the second last pet, etc., for now. Focus on understanding the "why" behind their actions. What were their struggles? What job were they trying to get done?

- **Use the six core insights as your guide: job, alternatives, struggles, segment, category, and triggers.** These insights form the bedrock of your quest to stand out.

- **Get scrappy or die trying.** You can mine reviews, join communities, talk to competitors' clients, or become a customer yourself, even if you have no existing business.

- **Obsess over finding recurring themes.** Then trust your instinct and move on to Stage 2.

At the end of this stage, you should have an idea of the main themes that came up across the six core insights. If you haven't done so already, use Table 3.6 (repeated here from above) as a template.

Table 3.6. Pattern Template

	Theme A	Theme B	...	Theme X
1. Job				
2. Alternatives				

	Theme A	Theme B	. . .	Theme X
3. Struggles				
4. Segment				
5. Category				
6. Triggers				

But, perhaps more importantly, you should start feeling this wave of clarity coming over you. All right, we're ready to move on to the next stage: **unique positioning.**

STAGE 2

Unique Positioning

April 19, 2017, 6:01 p.m.

I couldn't fucking believe he showed up.

There I was, crammed into the meeting room of my coworking space. A cheap Ikea table sat on top of the room's regular table, barely big enough for my stuff: my laptop, a $30 microphone, and the Skype window glowing on my screen.

On the other side, a legend: Seth Godin. (See Figure S2.1.) *The Purple Cow* guy. The marketer who made me love marketing. I read all his books and followed his blog posts every day. And now here he was, about to be on *my* little podcast, *Everyone Hates Marketers.*

Figure S2.1. Seth Godin (right) and myself (left).

He wore his usual purple glasses, and behind him was a bookshelf stacked high. I was about to hit "Record." No turning back now. *Just go with the flow,* I told myself. *He's just a regular guy.*

12 minutes later

Time flew by. Fuck.

He's good. I tried really hard to challenge him and get super practical, and he delivered. Nothing seemed to throw him off.

9 minutes later

Seth was talking about his usual message—companies need to stop racing to the bottom, trying to be the cheapest, and making average stuff for average people—when a thought popped into my head. I decided to just go for it.

"Seth," I said, "internet providers seem to always race to the bottom. They all compete on price. They have the same features. Let's say we have a brilliant idea of starting our own internet company. We provide internet just like the others. How would you make it remarkable?"

A small grin appeared on his face as I finished the question. "You asked the question exactly the wrong way," he replied. "I don't know if you did that on purpose."

Thanks for giving me the benefit of the doubt, Seth, but no.

Me, laughing nervously: "Haha. Nope."

Maybe I shouldn't have gone off-script. Stick to the plan, Louis; stick to the fucking plan.

Seth continued, "You can't begin by asking, 'How do we make it just like the others **and** make it remarkable?' You have to ask, 'How do we make it different from the others so it is remarkable?'"

Present day, seven years later

Looking back, this moment impacted me more than any other interviews I had ever run. And judging by the 300,000+ views on YouTube and the flood of comments—see Figure S2.2.—it wasn't just me who felt the impact.

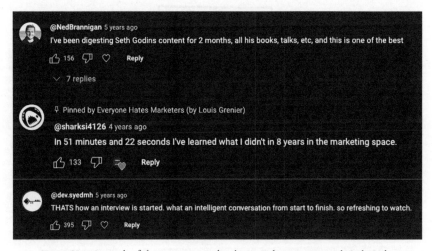

Figure S2.2. A sample of the comments under the YouTube interview with Seth Godin.

I'm so glad I ended up asking this clumsy question, because it sent me on a seven-year quest—one that slowly took over my life, even if Seth never intended it to.

"How do we make it different from the others so that it is remarkable?" Or, to use today's lingo, "How do you stand the f*ck out, like, for real?" I became obsessed with finding the answer.

Everyone explains being remarkably different is critical . . . and yet . . . I couldn't find *any* practical guidance. Not in business books, not in podcast interviews, and not in marketing courses. *Rien du tout!* It pissed me off . . .

Like being told to draw an owl without ever having seen one. Consider the next three stages to be your step-by-step guide to draw that owl.

It all starts with a **unique positioning.** This means understanding how you address customer challenges that others might overlook. You'll also craft a straightforward statement that describes how you're uniquely positioned to attract the right people, using **job, alternatives, struggles, segment,** and **category** as your foundation (see Figure S2.3). Having this statement is *really* useful for getting everyone on the same page both inside and outside your company.

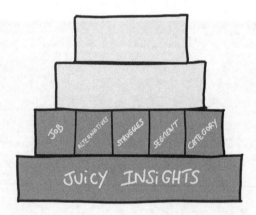

Figure S2.3. The five core insights of unique positioning.

4

The Job and the Alternatives

Let's go back to the example I used during my interview with Seth: internet providers. As he pointed out, you can't expect to create an internet company just like the others *and then* try to market it differently. That's being different for the sake of it.

People don't care about that. **When folks are buying stuff, they're *not* actively seeking out differences between them.**[22] **Instead, they're focused on reaching a job within the specific context they find themselves in.**

In the case of our new internet company, people don't wake up thinking, "Let's find a company that offers high-speed broadband differently today!" So there's no point in shouting about how *unique* we are. It doesn't matter if what we came up with is objectively *different* if customers don't care about that difference.

---

22 "Systematic study across product and service categories, countries, survey methods and questions types reveals two robust patterns: (1) Buyers of a brand perceive very weak differentiation yet this does not stop them loyally buying a particular brand. (2) A brand's level of perceived differentiation is very similar to their rivals." Learn more about perceived differentiation versus meaningful differentiation in Chapter 8 of Byron Sharp's book, *How Brands Grow: What Marketers Don't Know.* Oxford University Press, 2010.

The Problem: Being Different for the Sake of It Is a Fool's Errand

In slightly other words, being different for the sake of being *different* is a fool's errand. Instead, you must find a way to make that difference *meaningful* to your **segment**—a compelling reason to be picked that's been overlooked by **alternatives**. This is where you may find new market space, and this is how you can win as an underdog.

In the case of the internet company, we would first identify issues that people truly care about but aren't being addressed well. Then we would either position an existing product or create something new that solves these problems effectively and in a way that's in demand.

The Solution: Find Ignored Struggles

To make a meaningful difference for a specific group of people so they pick you, the key is to identify struggles your segment really wants to solve but that alternatives don't solve well or just ignore completely.

> I call them **ignored struggles.** They are the *super-frustrating* problems that prevent a certain group of people from getting a **job** done, which the competition isn't solving well.

By finding these, you offer something meaningful to your audience, giving them a reason to choose you over others. This is crucial because the odds are against you—you're not really supposed to win. You must control what you can and leave *nothing* to chance.

Example:

Take the example of the organic shampoo for Latinas. The founders, experienced beauty industry executives, noticed there were no household hair care brands designed specifically for Latinas and their curly hair—*pelo rizado*—that was *very* difficult to control.

How difficult? See for yourself with those real quotes from the customer interviews:

- "My hair is like lo mein noodles; there are times when I go outside and I look like a witch."

- "Never in my life was I able to weigh my hair down enough and control the frizz."

- "I was bullied as a child for ugly hair. My mom did not take the time to fix it. And now I want long hair and it takes two hours. I am waiting for a miracle because I would love to have bouncy curls."

- "Here in Miami we suffer with the heat and humidity. I have complicated hair: frizzy hair on top but not on the bottom. And then, one side is OK but the other side is terrible."

Can you feel their *immense* frustration? The vivid, almost visceral, language they're using? This perfectly illustrates an **ignored struggle**; a super-frustrating problem that existing solutions don't cater to. And it's easy to imagine how developing a solution to actually solve this "lo mein noodles" hair would be appealing for Latinas.

To get to the **ignored struggles**, we first need to know the exact goal the people in our **segment** want to reach (the **job**). This helps us find what's stopping them from achieving it. And then we need to look at the other options to see which ones aren't working well for them (the **alternatives**).

The Job

> The **job** is about your **segment's** goals, not your own. It forces you to stop looking at your belly button and start looking at your people's belly buttons.

The **job** is also a critical ingredient in decision-making. Without it, your **segment** could be "in pain" without doing anything about it. As Job to be Done theorist Alan Klement explains, "Imagine you're in a raft, lost in the middle of the ocean. It's an uncomfortable situation, but unless you make a choice on a direction to go or some way to get yourself out of it, you'll just continue floating aimlessly."[23]

In other words, your hair can be frizzy and out of control, but it's only becoming top-of-mind when you know you're going out this weekend. Unless you have a direction to go, you won't bother sorting it out. For this reason, we first need to find the job, which is the goal that people want to achieve so they know which direction they want to go.

There are three ground rules to give you the best chance to extract juicy insights about our **job**.

---

23   Louis Grenier and Alan Klement. 2018. "Why the Jobs to Be Done Framework Creates Better Products." *Everyone Hates Marketers.* https://podcast.everyonehatesmarketers.com/episodes/ why-the-jobs-to-be-done-framework-creates-better-products-alan-klement.

First, the job you pick must be specific enough to be within your control (or whatever area of focus is picked in Chapter 1). That's important because you do *not* want to promise the moon or find problems that you *cannot* do anything about. Also, a job that's too narrow might make you miss valuable **ignored struggles** that are part of the bigger picture.

For example, in 2017 I was hired by Hotjar, a web analytics company, to lead its content marketing. I later transitioned to a product marketing role to refine the company's positioning and help the business . . . well, stand the f*ck out. One of the first decisions we made was to describe the main **job** as "understand user behavior" instead of "increase online conversions." Why? Because increasing conversions was outside our direct control. Hotjar simply helped customers understand user activity on their websites. It was up to these customers to use those insights to improve user experience and potentially boost conversion rates.

Second, when defining the job, resist the urge to mention specific solutions, technologies, or tools. That's because solutions come and go, but the job is forever, since humans' core desires are not going to change anytime soon. This means it becomes your *raison d'être*: the reference point guiding all your efforts. For instance, humans have always wanted to connect with loved ones (the **job**), but a few thousand years ago, we were sending love letters on clay tablets—not in the form of disappearing digital messages.

And finally, phrase the job using the customer's language, starting with an action verb (like "stand the f*ck out" or "plan family vacation"). That's because the **job** is an active process, and verbs imply action and intent. And also, using the words the people in your **segment** use ensures you keep your eyes on their belly buttons instead of yours.

The Alternatives

Knowing what **alternatives** your customers have in mind is crucial. It helps us figure out if a particular **struggle** is being ignored and reveals our meaningful difference in the market.

There's one thing to remember when finding out what you really compete against: open your *chakras* and look beyond your immediate industry. You want to think broadly about the different ways people might get the **job** done.

Figure 4.1. Roger the Rooster looking beyond his immediate industry.

Remember the Latinas struggling to control their hair? They didn't just try other shampoos (the direct competition). They also mentioned going through a "two-hour hair care routine with rollers and a blowdry," and "going to a Dominican salon because no one else in NYC knows how to treat my hair," and just "trying all shampoos that seem natural." Notice how those other options go beyond the shampoo industry to touch on indirect competition and makeshift solutions.

The Plan: Find Out What You Really Compete Against

To get to the **ignored struggles**, we first need to know the exact goal the people in our **segment** want to reach (the **job**). This helps us find what's stopping them from achieving it. Then we need to look at the other options to see which ones aren't working well for them (the **alternatives**).

Step 1. Identify the Job

Now it's time to take your basket full of insights, lay them all out on the kitchen table, and identify the **job**—the specific goal your people want to achieve (like controlling the frizz).

To do so, go back to the patterns you've found in Chapter 3 for the **job**. Start with the theme that's been the most mentioned, and then pick the one that feels most essential and gives you the most direct influence over the outcome.

Example:

Imagine you've been hired as a marketing consultant for a company selling single-use packets to pour in the toilet before you, well, make a deposit. It's a simple product: open the packet and pour its contents directly into the surface of the toilet bowl; within seconds, essential oils will disperse into the air. Let's take a quick look at customer reviews (and use our intuition) to find out the main **job** that this product is "hired" to do. Also see Table 4.1.

- "I love these! I mostly use them when visiting someone's house, and it does what it's supposed to do: mask the odor. There may be a slight citrusy scent left in the air, but it's so subtle, and at least it's eliminating the unpleasant odor. I also love this product because the packets are small and discreet."

- "It's portable, discreet, and leak-proof. It covers odor without being overwhelmingly chemical or sweet. Excellent for hotels and workplaces, and any other shared bathroom situation. I would order it again."So, what specific goal do those customers want to achieve when buying this product? Table 4.1 sums up the potential jobs.

Table 4.1. Evaluating Potential Jobs for the Toilet Packet Product

Potential Jobs	Comments
Discreetly mask bathroom odors.	It doesn't start with a verb. It includes a specific way to reach that **job** ("discreetly").
Eliminate the unpleasant odor thanks to essential oils.	It includes a specific way to reach that **job** ("thanks to essential oils") that might change over time.
Prevent the spread of disease.	The product can't directly influence it (it's not a disinfectant).
Mask bathroom odors.	Bingo! It starts with a verb, is centered on what the product does, does not include any specifics about the methods used, and is stable over time.

TAKE ACTION

Identify the job—the specific goal your segment wants to achieve.

1. **Review your insights.** Review the data you've collected about your chosen area of focus (from Stage 1).

2. **Identify the goal.** Look for recurring themes and phrases in customers' own language.

3. **Keep it specific.** The job should be a clearly defined goal that your work can *directly* impact, but avoid getting so narrow that you miss out on the bigger picture.

4. **Focus on the "what."** Avoid mentioning specific solutions or technologies. The **job** is timeless; solutions change.

5. **Use the segment's language.** Phrase the **job** using your audience's words and phrases.

My area of focus' **job** is: _____.

Step 2. Find Out What You Really Compete Against

We know what people want to achieve, and now we can examine the other solutions they might have considered to get that job done. We're looking for **alternatives**—the different paths or solutions available to the **segment**, like going through a two-hour hair care routine with rollers and a blow dry (to control the frizz).

Go back to the patterns you've found in Chapter 3 for the **alternatives**. What are the most frequently mentioned solutions, competitors, or DIY approaches that pop up?

Example:

Let's go back to our toilet packet client. We know that people buy this product to mask bathroom odors—that's the **job**. But what **alternatives** are we *really* competing against?

Without looking at customer data, my mind goes straight to this *Dumb and Dumber* scene where Harry gets a stomach ache from accidentally drinking rat poison and ends up in his date's super-fancy bathroom. He's desperate to open the window for air but triggers a whole bunch of other bathroom functions like the bidet, fan, and shower.

This is relevant because "opening the bathroom window" could indeed be a good way to mask odors, just like "using perfume" or "avoiding going to the toilet altogether" (until we feel more at ease).

Now let's take a look at a few more customer reviews to extract the right **alternative**. (See Table 4.2.)

- "My granddaughter was happy to find these among her Christmas gifts. **The usual purse-type spray bottles** for use in public restrooms always seem to run out quickly or clog and not spray correctly. These are flat so fit anywhere—tiny purse or pant pocket and work every time."

- "**Poo Pourri** technically has an on-the-go product, but it's just a slightly **smaller version of their regular spray bottles**, which means it's still too clunky and doesn't fit in a small purse. Anyway, I highly recommend this product."

- "This product is very convenient and very discreet. Makes the room smell really nice but not overpowering. It has always been a **part of my travel "Poop Kit," which contains paper toilet seats and flushable sanitary wipes in a tiny wet-proof bag.** I highly recommend this product."

Table 4.2. Evaluating Potential Alternatives for the Toilet Packet Product

Potential Alternatives	Comments
Other scent packet products	**Incorrect.** Direct competitors are the obvious answer when considering **alternatives,** but in this case, the data does not support this.
Opening the bathroom window	**Incorrect.** Even though my mind went straight to the *Dumb and Dumber* scene, the data doesn't seem to support this.
Using portable spray bottles	**Correct.** It's the most mentioned **alternative** by a long mile.

The most frequently mentioned **alternative** is *using portable spray bottles.* They're not direct competitors to our packet since they're not in the exact same **category,** but they are competitors nonetheless as they're purchased for the same **job.**

TAKE ACTION

To uncover the real **alternatives** your customers consider or use already:

1. **Review your insights.** Go back to the data you've collected about your chosen area of focus (from Stage 1). What solutions are they comparing you with? What else did they try before you?

2. **Open your chakras and look beyond your industry.** What other ways do people solve the same problem? Think broader **categories** and even DIY solutions.

3. **Prioritize.** Which alternatives pop up most frequently? Which ones resonate with your target audience? Focus on those.

My top three **alternatives** are:

1. _____

2. _____

3. _____

Phew.

You've already accomplished a lot in this chapter. You've identified the **job**—the specific thing people are "hiring" you to do. This gives you direction and an end goal. Knowing that end goal helps you identify the **struggles** that prevent people from reaching it. You've also uncovered the **alternatives**—the other things people try in order to get that job done.

You might be tempted to rush ahead, but please, please, please . . . pause for a second.

Unearthing those two insights is not a small feat. It's fucking amazing, in fact. They are the very foundation of standing the f*ck out. So don't rush the process; it's worth it.

The Doubts: "I Have Too Many Alternatives to Choose From!"

"I have too many alternatives to choose from. How do I prioritize the top ones?"

It's easy to feel swamped when faced with a mountain of **alternatives**. In addition to focusing on how often each one comes up, prioritize by "threat" level. That's because "the threat from competitors is largely a matter of size," says marketing effectiveness expert Les Binet. "Your biggest competitors will be the biggest brands in the market."[24]

If the **alternatives** go beyond typical competitors and include things like work-arounds or DIY solutions, try grouping similar options together. And when in doubt, trust your instincts, *bien sûr*.

Finally, be careful not to introduce **alternatives** your customers do not mention because you are solving an irrelevant problem in their eyes.

"Can 'doing nothing' be considered an alternative?"

Oui . . . et non. Let me explain.

Imagine talking to someone with uncontrollable frizzy hair who would benefit from the specialist shampoo César and his team developed. After a couple of questions, you realize that this person is not really bothered by it and has never taken any particular step to get her mane under control. It's pretty obvious, since this person hasn't even considered investing the time, effort, or money to work on her hair, that "doing nothing" isn't really an **alternative** you need to worry about.

However, suppose that same person tells you she's thought about getting her hair under control for years. She tried several specialist shampoos and went to a couple of different hairdressers—but ended up going back to . . . doing nothing because nothing worked. Then yes, "doing nothing" becomes a valid **alternative** in her mind. She's already dipped her toes in the water, and you have evidence of it.

---

24 Les Binet and Sarah Carter. *How Not to Plan: 66 Ways to Screw It Up.* Troubador Publishing Limited, 2018.

The Recap: Lo Mein Noodles and Ignored Struggles

Remember the Latina women and their "lo mein noodles" hair? They craved a solution to their ignored **struggle**—uncontrollable frizz. In this chapter, we've identified the specific **job** your product or service does and the **alternatives** people are already using (or not using). This gives you a clear path to position your offering as the right solution.

Let's recap the key takeaways from this chapter:

- **Don't be different for the sake of it.** Find a meaningful difference that solves an ignored **struggle** for your **segment**.

- **The job is the specific goal the people in your segment want to achieve (e.g., "mask bathroom odors").** Keep it specific, timeless, and in their language.

- **Think beyond direct competitors with alternatives.** What other solutions, work-arounds, or DIY approaches do people use to get the job done (e.g., "portable spray bottles" for masking odors)?

- **Prioritize alternatives by threat level.** Focus on the most frequently mentioned and those posed by bigger players in the market.

- **"Doing nothing" can be a valid alternative if customers have actively considered and rejected other solutions.**

5

The Ignored Struggles

Humans tend to see themselves as perfectly *rational* creatures, but if that were the case, we would all live in harmony, and things like makeup, megayachts, or civet poop coffee[25] wouldn't exist.

Oui, oui. Civet poop coffee is a real thing.

And yes, it's exactly what you think it is: coffee beans that have been partially digested by the common palm civet—a teeny-weeny nocturnal mammal native to Southeast Asia—and then pooped out. And, of course, yes, it costs $650 per kilogram (instead of around $5 for "normal" coffee). Oh, and yes, people do buy it even though it's super unethical since civets are often caged and force-fed the beans, disrupting their natural diets and behaviors.

Civet coffee producers' *rational* argument is that it's more aromatic and less bitter than regular coffee. They also say that the beans wild civets pick are the best because civets would pick the ripest and tastiest coffee cherries.[26] But let's be real—if we were all ruled by logic, civet poop producers would be out of a job. Nobody really *needs* coffee shat out by a jungle cat.

---

25 "Kopi luwak." Wikipedia. https://en.wikipedia.org/wiki/Kopi_luwak.

26 Thank you Febriana Isnaini for adding this argument.

But people *want* it. They want it for *irrational* reasons.

Like, I'm sure it makes for a really good dinner party trick. You present your guests with a special, intriguing coffee. After each sip, you observe their reactions, waiting for the perfect moment to reveal your secret: "It's poop coffee! And I bought 50 grams of it for $49!" It's your way to impress others, to be seen as sophisticated and interesting, and to entertain your guests.

Or maybe it's to offer as a gift to your cousin Jason, who's a coffee lover. Or satisfy your curiosity by trying the world's most expensive coffee. Or maybe it's to relive memories from the past since you tasted it 28 years ago on a trip to Indonesia and you've been craving it ever since.

The Problem: We Love to Pretend People Are Robots

The folks who make up the marketing world love to pretend people are robots—cold, calculating machines that analyze every purchase with the logic of a cyborg. And who can blame them? It seems easier to sell to walking spreadsheets than to messy, emotional humans.

But it's just so fucking boring.

I don't want to live in a world where civet coffee is marketed as a tastier coffee, do you? I want to live in a world where it's positioned as a cool party trick for weirdos like me. Now that sounds fun, doesn't it?

All right . . . let's ditch the boring, robotic marketing formulas and dive headfirst into the fascinating world of human behavior—the real kind. Table 5.1 lists potential irrational reasons why folks would buy civet coffee.

Table 5.1. Breaking Down the Irrational Reasons Why People Would Buy Civet Poop Coffee

Irrational Reasons	Explanation
To use as a party trick to impress guests	People want to seem cool and interesting by serving fancy coffee.
To gift to a coffee lover	Giving this coffee shows you put in extra effort to find something really unique and expensive.
To satisfy people's curiosity by trying to find the world's most expensive coffee	People are curious about rare and exclusive things, even if they aren't better.
To relive memories from the past	Tasting it again can bring back happy feelings from a past experience.

The Solution: Start With Irrational Struggles

In the words of Seth Godin: "When in doubt, assume that people will act according to their current irrational urges, ignoring information that runs counter to their beliefs, trading long-term for short-term benefits, and being influenced by the culture they identify by. I'm not rational, and neither are you."[27]

All those reasons to want this weird coffee are caused by **irrational struggles**. By "irrational," I mean the bizarre stuff humans do that doesn't make sense.

---

27 Seth Godin. *This Is Marketing: You Can't Be Seen Until You Learn to See.* Penguin Publishing Group, 2018.

> **Irrational struggles** are the emotional and often subconscious problems that prevent a certain group of people from getting a **job** done.

This kind of struggle is the juiciest because the big companies you're likely competing against tend to see people as rational decision-makers—which means that they overlook the irrationality of human behavior.

And, honestly? I find this whole irrationality thing way more interesting than near-robotic logic. I like connecting with people on a deeper, more human level.

In most places, "you can never be fired for being logical," argues Rory Sutherland. "If your reasoning is sound and unimaginative, even if you fail, you will unlikely attract much blame." But solving rational problems will get you "exactly in the same place as your competitors."[28] **In other words, to find ignored struggles, start with the irrational ones.** Table 5.2 presents a list of **irrational struggles** I use with my clients when they're feeling stuck.

Table 5.2. Breaking Down Irrational Struggles

Irrational Struggle Category	Definition	Example
Self-love	Avoiding feeling like a loser	**LatinUs Beauty shampoo:** "My hair is like lo mein noodles. There are times when I go outside and I look like a witch."
Love and company	Avoiding loneliness	**PTDC online training:** "Jacked nerds" feel the need to be surrounded by others like them to grow their business.

---

28 Rory Sutherland. *Alchemy: The Surprising Power of Ideas That Don't Make Sense.* Ebury Publishing, 2019.

Irrational Struggle Category	Definition	Example
Fitting in	Craving approval and belonging	**Toilet packet:** "I bought these because now I have a roommate. We have to share a bathroom, so I can discreetly keep these packets in my container and use them when I'm home and won't be embarrassed when my roommate walks in after."
Purpose	Seeking meaning, unity, and nostalgia	**Civet coffee:** Reliving memories after tasting it 28 years ago on a trip to Indonesia
Control freaks	Controlling and organizing chaos	**LatinUs Beauty shampoo:** "Never in my life have I been able to weigh my hair down enough and control the frizz."
Fewer decisions	Avoiding overwhelming choices	**This book:** Gives readers a comprehensive plan to follow to stand the f*ck out
Entertainment	Seeking fun and avoiding boredom	**East Forged cold brew tea:** Treating myself to a fancy drink after a long day
"Look at me!"	Seeking recognition and wanting to be valued	**Civet coffee:** To use as a party trick to impress guests
Reducing risk	Reducing risk, even if it means not using the best option	**Hotjar behavior analytics tool:** Signing up to use the tool because you've come across it in a previous role

Irrational Struggle Category	Definition	Example
Power trip	Seeking superiority or at least "keeping up with the Joneses"	**LatinUs Beauty shampoo:** Looking the best when going out with friends

On the other hand, there are the rational struggles that we all tend to think about easily. Table 5.3 shows the rational factors people think about when making choices and what we, marketers, tend to think about naturally.

Table 5.3. Breaking Down Rational Struggles

Rational Struggles	Definition
Knowledge	Getting smarter
Safety	Feeling safe and secure
Health	Staying healthy and avoiding pain
Time	Saving time and avoiding wasting it
Money	Making money and avoiding losing it
Tranquility	Reducing effort and avoiding hassle

Whether **struggles** are rational or irrational, the underlying structure remains the same. **Use the SOS framework to make these insights easily shareable with your team or clients and create a shared understanding (Figure 5.1).** It stands for:

- **Stop.** Do they want to stop, avoid, or change something?
- **Obstacle.** What is standing in the way of reaching the **job**, exactly?
- **Situation.** In what context does this **struggle** typically occur?

Figure 5.1. Use the SOS framework to structure your struggles.

For example, *avoiding being embarrassed when my roommate walks in the bathroom after me* is a good way to use the SOS framework because it clearly describes the direction (stop), the obstacle (embarrassment), and the situation (when my roommate walks in the bathroom after me).

To avoid confusing **struggles** with **jobs**, think of it like friends in a raft navigating a river, as beautifully illustrated in Figure 5.2. The **job** is to reach the beach on the other side, while the **struggles** are the rocks in the way. Clearly define each obstacle using the SOS framework to identify the perceived fears, risks, obstacles, or lack of resources preventing them from reaching their goal.

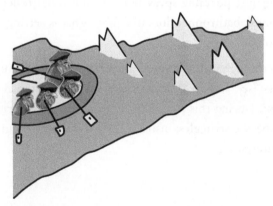

Figure 5.2. Roger the Rooster and his friends want to avoid the rocks (struggles) in order to reach the beach (job).

The Plan: Find Problems Others Have Overlooked

Remember, in this chapter, we're on a quest to uncover **ignored struggles**—the super-frustrating problems that prevent a certain group of people from getting a **job** done, which the competition isn't solving well.

Step 1. List All the Struggles

OK, first, list your audience's **struggles**—rational and, of course, irrational. Remember those **jobs** and **alternatives** we talked about earlier? This is where they come in handy.

Go back to the patterns you've found in Chapter 3 for the **struggles**. Look at the themes you've identified—starting with the most common ones—and dig deep: What is preventing customers from getting the **job** done? What problems are **alternatives** ignoring?

Go wild because meaningful differences emerge in granular, specific struggles. What you might dismiss as insignificant could be the key to unlocking a powerful **insight**. Resist the urge to merge **struggles**.

Example:

Let's go back to our toilet packet example. We know that we're really competing against **portable spray bottles**—not other toilet packets—to help people **mask bathroom odors** (the **job**). What is getting in the way of getting the **job** done?

Let's scan through the customer data we've collected during the **insight foraging** stage (see Table 5.4). In our case, we used customer reviews as a starting point. During this step, I try to avoid being too scientific about identifying specific **struggles**; instead, I like to follow my gut when I spot something interesting.

Table 5.4. Struggles for Toilet Packet

Struggle	Quote	Type of Struggle
Avoid spending so much effort to mask odors.	"Instead of having to bend over and spray the toilet strategically, all I have to do is open a small packet and pour it in the toilet. The bathroom instantly smells gorgeous, and any sort of poop smell is nonexistent."	**Control freaks:** Controlling and organizing chaos **Fewer decisions:** Avoiding overwhelming choices
Avoid getting bored with one type of scent.	"I actually really like the lemony scent it leaves when you first pour it."	**Entertainment:** Seeking fun and avoiding boredom
Reduce the risk of others finding I've gone number two when using the product.	"I didn't have to worry about hearing that "spritz" sound, which I was a bit self-conscious about."	**Control freaks:** Controlling and organizing chaos **Reducing risk:** Even if it means forgoing the best option
Reduce the risk of getting embarrassed when living with others.	"I bought these because now I have a roommate. We have to share a bathroom so I can discreetly keep these packets in my container and use them when I'm home and won't be embarrassed when my roommate walks in after."	**Reducing risk:** Even if it means forgoing the best option **Fitting in:** Craving approval and belonging
Avoid running out of product when I need it most.	"The usual purse-type spray bottles for use in public restrooms always seem to run out quickly."	**Tranquility:** Reducing effort and avoiding hassle

Struggle	Quote	Type of Struggle
Ensure my bottle's cool design doesn't get ignored when I'm with friends.	"The bottle has a fun design, and funny poems to describe the spray's function and uses."*	**"Look at me!"**: Seeking recognition and wanting to be valued
Reduce the risk of leakage and spills in bags.	"Unlike the sprays, it will not spill (yes, even when in a baggie) all over my handbag and ruin it."	**Tranquility:** Reducing effort and avoiding hassle
Avoid leaving an overpowering scent taking over the bathroom.	"It didn't leave a heavy perfume scent; it was more of an extremely light, almost faint, lemon/mint scent."	**Control freaks:** Controlling and organizing chaos
Stop feeling insecure when I need to go to the bathroom.	"Def feel more confident going to the bathroom when I have to go"	**Self-love:** Avoiding feeling like a loser **Tranquility:** Reducing effort and avoiding hassle
Avoid getting stopped by airport security when going on a trip.	"In preparation for a trip to Europe, we went searching for a portable, nonleaking, lightweight toilette fragrance that would pass TSA restrictions."	**Tranquility:** Reducing effort and avoiding hassle **Time:** Saving time and avoiding wasting it

*I'm using a review from an **alternative** here, which is as valid to uncover **struggles**.

I'm sure I could find more, but this is good enough for a first pass to quickly find opportunities to stand the f*ck out.

TAKE ACTION

It's not enough to know what your customers want; you need to understand what's *stopping* them from getting it. Dive deep into their **struggles**—both rational and irrational—to find juicy insights.

Here's what to do:

1. **Revisit your jobs and alternatives.** Remember the patterns you identified in Chapter 3? Use them as a starting point to brainstorm **struggles** related to each **job** and its **alternatives**.

2. **Dig deep.** For each theme, ask: *What obstacles prevent customers from achieving their goal? What issues are competitors ignoring?*

3. **Get super specific.** The tiniest frustrations can lead to the biggest "aha" moments. Resist the urge to combine **struggles**; list each one separately.

Full list of **struggles**:

- _____
- _____
- _____
- _____

Step 2. Identify the Most Promising Struggles

OK, at this stage, you have a list of **struggle** statements you've made based on the insights you gathered. But you may not have a clear idea of the ones that you should zero in on. **Remember, we want to find the most** *frustrating, intense* **problems in order to have the highest chance of getting noticed and picked by the people we seek to serve.**

How do we find them? **We look for the ones that pop up again and again.** We'll rely on the frequency of those **struggles** to guide us. But frequency isn't enough. We also want the **struggles** that hit them where it hurts—the frustrating ones that leave them feeling stuck. Table 5.5 shows the two criteria you can use to identify promising **struggles**.

Table 5.5. Criteria to Identify Promising Struggles

Criteria	What It Is	How to Spot It
Frequency	The more frequently a **struggle** is mentioned, the more widespread and impactful addressing it is likely to be.	Look for the number of mentions in your data.
Frustration	How critical is it for folks to solve this **struggle**? Is it a minor annoyance or a major blocker to achieving their goals?	Look for statements that attribute the decision to solving this specific **struggle**. Watch out for emotional language, curse words, and any other colorful evidence.

For frequency, please don't obsess over counting mentions like, "This one came up 19 times! This one 18!" Don't get *too* scientific. Think of it as high, medium, or low.

For frustration, ask yourself: *How frustrated are people with this particular struggle? Is it mildly annoying or a major roadblock?* I like to think of it as a hurdle race: the finish line is the **job** and the hurdles are the **struggles** you have to jump over. The higher the hurdle, the more effort is required to clear it, and the more frustrated we become. It's the same with **struggles**.

Example:

Continuing our odor-masking example, let's plot each of the **struggles** we've identified against the two criteria mentioned previously and create a scorecard, depicted in Table 5.6.

Table 5.6. Struggle Scorecard

Struggle	Frequency	Frustration
Avoid spending so much effort to mask odors.	High	High
Avoid getting bored with one type of scent.	Low	Low
Reduce the risk of others finding I've gone number two when using the product.	Medium	High
Reduce the risk of getting embarrassed when living with others.	Low	High
Avoid running out of product when I need it most.	Low	Medium
Make sure the cool design on my bottle doesn't get ignored when I'm with friends.	Low	Low
Reduce the risk of leakage and spills in bags.	Medium	Medium
Avoid leaving an overpowering scent taking over the bathroom.	Medium	Medium
Stop feeling insecure when I need to go to the bathroom.	High	High
Avoid getting stopped by airport security when going on a trip.	Low	Low

And now let's focus only on the most common and frustrating **struggles** we've identified, as in Table 5.7. I've come up with three, but you may have more or less.

Table 5.7. Focusing on the Most Common and Frustrating Struggles

Struggle	Frequency	Frustration
Avoid spending so much effort to mask odors.	High	High
Reduce the risk of others finding I've gone number two when using the product.	Medium	High

Struggle	Frequency	Frustration
Stop feeling insecure when I need to go to the bathroom.	High	High

Et voilà! **We now have three struggles to plot against alternatives in order to identify the ones that are ignored.** Remember, this process isn't about achieving perfect objectivity. It's about prioritizing the insights that stand the f*ck out the most.

TAKE ACTION

Now it's time to zero in on the most frustrating problems you've encountered:

1. **Create a struggle scorecard.** Take the list of all the **struggles** you've identified in the previous step and assign *frequency* and *frustration* scores for each.

2. **Highlight the most promising ones.** Zoom in on the **struggles** with the highest scores.

Most promising **struggles**:

_____ (Frequency: _____, Frustration: _____)

_____ (Frequency: _____, Frustration: _____)

_____ (Frequency: _____, Frustration: _____)

_____ (Frequency: _____, Frustration: _____)

_____ (Frequency: _____, Frustration: _____)

Step 3. Identify Your Meaningful Differentiation

And now for the *pièce de résistance.* The holy grail of differentiation. Finding problems that the competition has overlooked: **ignored struggles.**

We're going to take your list of prioritized **struggles** and plot them against the **alternatives** you've identified in the previous chapter to uncover **ignored struggles**—the super-frustrating problems that prevent a certain group of people from getting a **job** done, which the competition isn't solving well.

To do so, let's plot the **struggles** you uncovered against the **alternatives** you identified earlier. A simple grid like Table 5.8 does the trick. Think of it as a matrix that reveals which **alternatives** effectively address each **struggle** ("Solved well") and which ones miss the mark entirely ("**Ignored**").

Table 5.8. Ignored Struggle Matrix

	Alternative 1	Alternative 2
Struggle A	Solved well	Solved well
Struggle B	Ignored	Ignored
Struggle C	Solved well	Ignored

In this fictional example, **struggle B** is ignored by both **alternatives 1** and **2**, which means that we've identified an **ignored struggle**—a real, truthful reason for the people you seek to serve to pick you over anyone else.

Example:

Let's use this simple grid in Table 5.9 for our toilet packet example. For the rows, I'm taking the most common and frustrating **struggles** we've found in the last step. For the columns, I'm taking the **alternative** we found in the last chapter.

Table 5.9. Ignored Struggle Matrix for Toilet Packet

	Alternative: Using portable spray bottles
Struggle: Avoid spending so much effort to mask odors.	**Ignored.** Customers report it covers the existing smell but doesn't *neutralize* it, and it takes too much effort to spray in "strategic" places.

	Alternative: Using portable spray bottles
Struggle: Reduce the risk of others finding I've gone number two when using the product.	**Ignored.** Some customers point out that the spritz noise of the bottle (and its potent aroma, probably) is a dead giveaway.
Struggle: Stop feeling insecure when I need to go to the bathroom.	**Ignored.** Confidence seems to be an issue for scent packet users and their reason for switching from spray bottles.

So there we have it.

After scanning through publicly available data (**insight foraging method 1** in this case) and digging deep inside my gray matter (which is method 3), I uncovered three **ignored struggles** to build our meaningful differentiation around.

It ain't much, but it's honest work.

TAKE ACTION

You've already laid the groundwork by identifying your customers' **struggles** and **alternatives**. Now it's time to pinpoint the **ignored struggles**.

Here's what to do:

1. **Create an ignored struggle matrix.** List your most common and frustrating **struggles** as rows and the top **alternatives** as columns.

2. **Assess each cell.** For each **struggle-alternative** combination, determine if the **alternative** effectively solves the **struggle** ("Solved well") or overlooks it ("**Ignored**").

3. **Highlight the ignored.** These are your **ignored struggles**—golden opportunities to make your offering stand the f*ck out.

Top **ignored struggles:**

1. _____

2. _____

3. _____

The Doubts: "My Struggles Are Too Vague!"

"Identifying a job sounds an awful lot like struggles. What's the difference between them?"

That's a good question . . . it tripped me up for the longest time, too. Think of the **job** as the big picture, the goal your customer wants to achieve. In our toilet scent packet example, *masking bathroom odors* is the **job** we've identified.

The **struggles** are the annoying obstacles in their way: the worry that guests will hold their breath (and their noses!), the fear that current solutions will just add to the smell, or the concern that the product will leak in their handbag and ruin everything. These are the things that make achieving that job with current **alternatives** difficult.

"I feel like the struggles I've identified are too generic. What should I do?"

If your research doesn't uncover many **struggles** or if you feel like they're just too generic, don't worry. I have a solution: breaking down your **job** into smaller steps using a **job** map. It's a chronological way to see how customers get the **job** done, from start to finish. It's not the same as a customer journey map because it's not about you and your solution; it's purely about the customers and *their* perspective.

A **job** map like the one in Table 5.10 hypothesizes that **job** execution has a universal structure that can be split into eight stages.

Table 5.10. Job Map for Toilet Packet

Stages	Definition	Mask Bathroom Odors (Job)
Define	Set goals and figure out how to get the **job** done.	Feel the need to go number 2.
Locate	Collect what's needed.	Find a toilet nearby Get my handbag.
Prepare	Get things ready.	Go to the toilet. Close the door.
Confirm	Ensure everything is ready.	Make sure my bottle spray is in my handbag.
Execute	Get the **job** done, as planned.	Spray strategically around the toilet. Place toilet paper in the bowl. Go about my business.

Stages	Definition	Mask Bathroom Odors (Job)
Monitor	Check if the job has been done as expected.	Check if the bad smells are gone. Flush the toilet.
Modify	Adjust approach if needed.	Spray again.
Conclude	End the job and follow up.	Dispose of the packaging. Wash hands.

See how breaking down the **job** into smaller ones helps to get more specific? It helps you to go one level deeper and find out what is specifically getting in the way of customers getting the **job** done.

"What if I can't find any ignored struggles? At least none big enough to warrant building a new solution?"

Don't hit the panic button just yet. It's very common to end up in this situation, especially on the first pass. Here's my advice:

- **Dig deeper into irrational struggles**—the ones nobody seems to be talking about. Maybe your colleagues, clients, or even competitors never mentioned any of them. So what? If your gut tells you there's something there, don't ignore it just to fit in.

- **Forage for more insights.** Revisit the first stage of the stand the f*ck out methodology and expand your research. Try new methods to talk to more people.

- **Go beyond the product.** If you're still feeling stuck after this, you might be in an incredibly mature market with an existing product that you can't change. In this case, pay particular attention to the job map so you can think about the entire experience surrounding your product.

Now let's address the elephant in the room. If you can't unearth **ignored struggles** after all that, it probably means that you're in a super-competitive market with no meaningful differentiation. In this case, developing a **distinctive brand** is your best bet to stand the f*ck out.

"How is this supposed to help us compete against big companies?"

The key word here is *specificity*. Make sure to pick a *specific* **job** and *specific* **struggles** in a *specific* context, something that big companies can't have on their radar because they're too big.

Also, those big companies tend to suffer from the same disease, which Youngmee Moon, author of *Different*, calls "augmentation-by-addition": "To the extent that a product can be thought as a set of benefits, product marketers will habitually look to improve it by bolstering those benefits. [. . .] It used to be that laundry detergent offered the regular promise of clean clothes; today, there is static elimination, stain protection, and fabric softening."

Finally, new **struggles** appear every day because of new technology, new contexts appearing, and so on. There's always something there.

"It's not going to last, because if I identify a meaningful differentiation, then maybe competitors will catch up."

Don't overestimate competitors. **Most of them will never read this book and care enough to think about standing the f*ck out.** They might copy your product/service or client's features, or the way you cater to your customers' needs, but you will always be one step ahead. Make those competitors followers.

The Recap: Who Buys Civet Poop Coffee?

Nobody needs civet poop coffee, but they want it for irrational reasons. Just like your customers want what you offer in part for irrational reasons. We've learned to let go of robotic marketing formulas and understand the real reasons people buy—their **irrational struggles.**

Let's recap the key takeaways from this chapter:

- **Humans are irrational.** Forget logic; tap into the emotional, sub-conscious desires driving your customers.

- **Unearth ignored struggles.** These are the frustrating problems your competitors overlook because they're too busy being rational.

- **Use the SOS framework.** Define **struggles** by what customers want to Stop, the Obstacle in their way, and the Situation where it occurs.

- **Prioritize struggles by frequency and frustration.** Focus on the problems that come up often and make people want to tear their hair out.

- **Map the job to uncover hidden struggles.** Break down the customer's journey into smaller steps to pinpoint specific pain points.

- **Tip: Don't be afraid to get granular.** The tiniest frustrations can lead to the biggest opportunities to stand the f*ck out.

6

The Segment

There's a French rapper who goes by the name "Orelsan." He's a white dude from Normandy, and he grew up in a typical town in the countryside of France, raised by parents who are teachers.

Not quite the average upbringing for a rapper, *n'est-ce pas?* Not to be cliché, but even in France rappers tend to be associated with gangsters, making it quite a dangerous career to break into.

Orelsan, meanwhile, rose to fame by rapping about a shitty life in a shitty town in the middle of nowhere. For example, in "Changement," the song that made him famous, he raps:[29]

> *Old folks don't understand what's going on in young people's heads*
> *They weren't raised by TV or by PlayStation*
> *They don't understand how messed up we are*
> *They don't know about the Internet, nightclubs, kebabs, DVDs*

---

29 Orelsan. 2011. "Changement [CLIP OFFICIEL]." YouTube. https://www.youtube.com/watch?v=lIIyA3DAQXo.

And you know what's funny . . . I, too, grew up in the French countryside, in a small village with 300 inhabitants. I, too, was raised by teachers. And I, too, hated living so far away from everything.

The beauty of Orelsan's rise to popularity is that he wasn't a marketer. He didn't follow this book's methodology, but he served a segment with an ignored struggle. Young French teens in the countryside didn't feel like there was any music for them. And he sang about their exact situations.

He could have tried to follow other rappers, writing about urban life, drugs, and violence, but he didn't. He focused on his own experiences and wrote for people facing challenges other rappers didn't talk about. His popularity shows the power of finding the right **segment**.

Mic drop

The Problem: Niching Down Is Just Too Restrictive

Ever heard a marketing guru scream about niching down until your ears bled? You know the ones: "Riches are in the niches." "Serve a niche within a niche." "Niche, niche, niche." They paint this picture of laser-focusing on a teeny-weeny slice of the market, usually defined by industry or demographics. It's enough to make you believe you need to squeeze yourself into a box labeled "Marketing Consultant for Left-Handed Chiropractors Who Treat Only Dachshunds."

But here's the thing: they're wrong. You're told to squeeze yourself into a box so small you can barely breathe while your creativity—and joy—dry up and die. You're not building a brand that stands the f*ck out; you're building a fucking cage.

That's why I believe the very concept of niching is a trap, like the one I drew in Figure 6.1. For example, I'm sure you've thought, *"My customers are all from different sectors. Different sizes. Different roles. I don't want to pick just one of them . . . This feels so fucking restrictive!"*

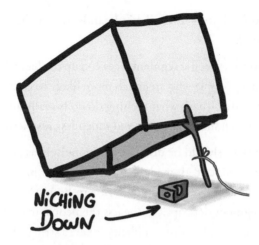

NiCHiNG DOWN ➔

Figure 6.1. Niching down is a trap.

Of course it feels restrictive . . . Just like advising Orelsan to write lyrics only for teenagers who are into street art. **The way you've been taught about choosing your niche is restrictive. Not only that, but thinking about it this way will likely prevent you from standing the f*ck out.**

So what if folks are not in the same industry? So what if they're not all Gen Z? So what if the decision-makers don't have the same job title?

All those attributes are *arbitrary*.

The Solution: Obsess Over One Segment

Orelsan didn't care whether his fans were Scorpio ascendant monkeys or practiced ventriloquism in their spare time. But he cared about young people living in boring, quiet suburbs who felt misunderstood and forgotten by other rappers (like younger me!).

A segment is a group of people you can serve in a way that gives you a distinct advantage[30] **against alternatives. The people in the segment have struggles in common that *only* you can solve in a specific way, which**

---

30 Louis Grenier and Adele Revella. 2018. "How to Create 100% Accurate and Detailed Buyer Persona." *Everyone Hates Marketers.* https://podcast. everyonehates marketers.com/episodes / how-to-create-100 -accurate-and-detailed-buyer-persona.

pulls them toward you—even if big brands are in the mix (or French gangsta rappers).

Obsessing over a specific **segment** frees you up to channel all your energy toward a group of people who are much more likely to care about what you have to say and offer. That's what niching down is really about. This way of thinking feels much more natural—and much less restrictive.

First, a segment should be described as concisely as possible. This may sound controversial, but after identifying **segments** more times than I've cooked mushroom risotto for my wife, I can honestly say that the *more* complex the **segment** description, the *less* the people in charge understand their customers. Why? Because simplicity is key: a straightforward **segment** description helps everyone—clients, colleagues, employees—understand, internalize, and remember it better.

For example, Orelsan's **segment** could be described as *Young French people living in boring, quiet suburbs who feel misunderstood and forgotten by other rappers.* Every single word in this description serves a purpose: it highlights the **ignored struggle** that Orelsan is solving (feeling misunderstood) for a specific group of people (young French people living in boring, quiet suburbs).

Second, and this is critical: don't obsess over finding superficial differences. It's easy to get caught up in the differences between your customers—like their industries (e.g., B2B tech versus retail), roles (e.g., marketing managers versus CEOs), demographics, or company sizes. Just because your customers come from different backgrounds doesn't mean your **segment** is too broad. Instead of fixating on the differences, focus on the *common ground*—a well-defined **segment** is built on shared **struggles**, not superficial differences.

For example, with LatinUs Beauty and its organic shampoo, it's rather easy to find superficial differences inside that simple **segment** description: *Latinas with long, frizzy hair living in humid weather (mainly Florida and California).* Looking back at their customer interviews, the folks at LatinUs can see that their customers ranged from 17 to 57, spanning four generations. But age doesn't affect their customers' desire for frizz control! Focusing on the shared **struggle** (frizzy hair) is critical, even with diverse demographics.

Third, focus only on the essential details that highlight your distinct advantage. Those details could be demographics (like age or occupation), firmographics (like, if we're selling to businesses, company size or their industry), and context (the specific circumstances that lead customers to take action)—as long as they highlight why these people are more inclined to choose us instead of anyone else.

For example, in 2017 I launched my *Everyone Hates Marketers* podcast to help tech *marketers* grow without resorting to shady tactics. However, I soon discovered that my audience wasn't defined by the demographics or firmographics I had expected.

Emails poured in from a diverse group: marketing creators, retail CMOs, Broadway producers, photographers, lawyers, even real estate agents. At first, this variety made me nervous. Wasn't I supposed to stick to a specific industry or job title? Then it hit me. While these listeners came from different backgrounds, they had something in common: they all wanted to promote themselves or their businesses but were uncomfortable with pushy marketing tactics. My podcast had a unique advantage in serving this group because it was the only one focused on people who were tired of aggressive growth strategies and wanted to grow by genuinely helping others.

As a summary, Table 6.1 shows examples of potential **segments** and evaluates if they are well described or fail to meet the criteria discussed previously.

Table 6.1. Evaluating Potential Segments

Potential Segments	Comments
LatinUs Beauty shampoo: Meet Sofia "Sunshine" Rodriguez, the vivacious 28-year-old Latina with a mane of wild, untamable curls that seem to have a life of their own. Living in the heart of Miami's Little Havana, Sofia embodies the spirit of her sun-soaked surroundings. By day, Sofia works as a yoga instructor and part-time salsa dance teacher, spreading joy and positive energy wherever she goes . . .	**Too much detail.** We're not writing a novel; we're identifying a group of people who are more likely to buy from us.
Everyone Hates Marketers **podcast:** Tech marketers	**Too little detail.** It's unclear how marketers working in tech would be more inclined to listen to my podcast over any other.
This book: I'm writing this book for Marketer Mary. • She is 41-year-old. • She is Scorpio ascendant with a fierce personality. • She has two kids, aged 7 and 5. • She lives in Boston. • She has limited vacation time. • She likes ice cream. Her favorite flavor is vanilla.	**Too much like a dating site.** None of this information will help you to motivate customers to buy. None of this information will help you fight FOMO and know precisely where to invest your marketing budget. None of this information will help you attract more customers or increase revenue.
Everyone Hates Marketers **podcast:** Folks sick of marketing bullshit who need to market themselves (to find a job, for example), their business (entrepreneurs in competitive markets), or someone else's business (folks who run marketing/create businesses, doing work with clients)	**Just right.** It includes just enough detail to make it specific, but not too much that it becomes overwhelming.

To sum up, your **segment** description should be a short sentence that contains the attributes linked to the **struggles** and the context in which these **struggles** occur.

The Plan: How to Find Your Segment

Throughout my career, I've discovered three powerful steps for obsessively identifying the group of people to focus on.

Step 1. Find People with Intense or Frequent Struggles

This technique focuses on identifying people who experience a particular struggle more *frequently* or *intensely* than the average person. Why? Because the more people struggle, the more likely they are to be receptive to solving their problems. To use a simple analogy, whom do you think struggles more with bug bites? Someone who got stung once by a mosquito or someone who got attacked by a swarm of bees? I've created Figure 6.2 to help you visualize this.

Figure 6.2. Getting stung by a mosquito or attacked by a swarm of bees.

By targeting these individuals, we increase our chances of reaching those who are most receptive to what we offer, which gives us an advantage over the top dogs.

I remember working with a client at Hotjar who offered an all-in-one solution for PDFs—converting, compressing, you name it. One of the biggest **struggles** the client tackled was the time and errors involved in converting PDFs to editable documents. **The client realized that administrative assistants, especially in high-pressure fields like law, felt this pain** *acutely.* **They were constantly converting scanned documents for edits and any mistake could have serious consequences.** The pressure to get it right and do it quickly made this struggle far more intense for them than for the average person.

Take each **ignored struggle** you've identified and consider who might experience it more intensely or frequently than average. Look beyond basic demographics to find meaningful attributes that make certain people more susceptible to these **struggles**. Look at Table 6.2 for examples.

Table 6.2. Segment Attributes

Attributes	Question	Example
Occupation/ Inudstry	Are certain jobs exposed to the **struggle** with more intensity?	**All-in-one tool for PDFs:** Administrative assistants in the Law sector are constantly converting scanned documents for edits, and any mistake could have serious consequences.
Company size/ Structure	Do certain types of companies **struggle** with it more?	**Hotjar behavior analytics tool:** Businesses that primarily rely on their website to generate revenue tend to care more about their conversion rate than the average.
Company revenue	Do Fortune 500 companies **struggle** with it more than a small mom-and-pop shop?	Nonprofits must maintain transparency with donors, which adds administrative complexity.

Attributes	Question	Example
Location	Can geographic location play a role in how intensely people experience **struggles**?	**LatinUs Beauty:** Folks living in warm/humid weather struggle to control their hair more often than the average.
Age/Life stage	Are specific age groups more prone to experiencing this **struggle** acutely?	Parents whose children have grown up and left home might struggle to find a new purpose.
Income level	Does income level make the **struggle** more difficult for some?	Wealthy families often struggle with complex dynamics when it comes to money matters, especially regarding who inherits what.
Education level	Do people with certain education levels encounter this **struggle** more severely?	Folks who've spent years collecting advanced degrees, might face an unexpected challenge when job hunting: employers often view candidates with multiple master's or PhDs as "overqualified."
Interests/ Hobbies	Are people with specific interests more likely to face certain **struggles**?	**PTDC fitness training:** "Jacked nerds" who train and go to the gym every day
Values/Beliefs	Can religious, political, or philosophical beliefs impact how intensely someone experiences a **struggle**?	Anarcho-primitivists believe that civilization should return to noncivilized ways of life. Living off the grid, for example, could pose legal issues for some.
Expertise level	Do novices or experts in a particular field encounter this **struggle** with different intensities?	**Civet coffee:** Coffee connaisseurs* might be more willing to discover new exotic tastes.
Health	Can health conditions make particular **struggles** more intense?	**East Forged cold brew tea:** Folks who want to stay sober while still treating themselves

Attributes	Question	Example
Family status	Can family circumstances affect how strongly someone feels a **struggle**?	New dads who struggle to maintain a consistent fitness routine

*I'm spelling it the French way. You can't stop me.

Don't limit yourself to the attributes listed above; feel free to brainstorm additional relevant characteristics. There are no right or wrong answers here. The purpose is to challenge your thinking. You can use the template in Table 6.3.

Table 6.3. Ignored Struggle/Segment Attribute Matrix

Attributes	Ignored Struggle 1	Ignored Struggle 2
Attribute A		
Attribute B		
Attribute C		

Example:

OK, I know you're dying for me to continue with my toilet packet example, so I must oblige. We have identified three **ignored struggles**. Now we want to identify the specific group of people we could serve in a way that gives us an advantage as underdogs. In Table 6.4, I've filled out the matrix with **segment** attributes as they relate to each **ignored struggle**.

Table 6.4. Ignored Struggle/Segment Attribute Matrix for
Toilet Packet

Attributes	Avoid spending so much effort to mask odors	Reduce the risk of others finding I've gone number two when using the product	Stop feeling insecure when I need to go to the bathroom
Occupation/ Industry	Jobs requiring frequent travel		
Company size/ Structure			
Company revenue			
Location			Job that requires working in an office with shared toilets
Age/Life stage	Younger folks who are active on the dating scene		
Income level			
Education level		First-year college students who have to share a room for the first time	
Interests/ Hobbies	People going out often	Cruise lovers	
Values/Beliefs	People who see cleanliness as non-optional		
Expertise level			

Attributes	Avoid spending so much effort to mask odors	Reduce the risk of others finding I've gone number two when using the product	Stop feeling insecure when I need to go to the bathroom
Health	Folks with digestive issues who need to go to the toilet often		
Family status			

We've identified characteristics common to people who might encounter certain bathroom difficulties more frequently than the average person. This suggests that these individuals could be more receptive to a solution like our toilet scent packet:

- Jobs requiring frequent travel
- Younger folks who are active on the dating scene
- People going out often
- People who see cleanliness as non-optional
- Folks with digestive issues who need to go to the toilet often
- First-year college students who have to share a room for the first time
- Cruise lovers
- Job that requires working in an office with shared toilets

This list looks random right now, but do not worry; we'll make sense of it soon.

TAKE ACTION

It's time to find the people who feel those **ignored struggles** most acutely. Here's what to do:

1. **Create an ignored struggle matrix.** Plot the attributes as rows and the **ignored struggles** as columns.

2. **Assess each cell.** For each attribute-**struggle** combination, see if you can think of specific characteristics that would make someone more likely to experience this **struggle** more frequently or intensely than the average. If yes, put down your thoughts in the table. If not, leave it blank. It's *alllllllll gooooood.*

List of meaningful attributes:

- _____
- _____
- _____
- _____
- _____

Step 2. Find People in a Specific Context

This method focuses on identifying people based on the specific circumstances—or triggers—that motivate them to take action. Why? Because understanding the context of someone's needs allows you to define your segment based on real-life situations, rather than *flavorless* demographics or company data. It's about understanding the *why* behind people's actions.

Even though we cover **triggers** in more detail in **Stage 4, "Continuous Reach,"** we're going to start diving into the concept now to add depth to our **segment**.

Go back to the **trigger** patterns you've found while foraging for **insights**. Look at the themes you've identified—starting with the most common ones—and dig deep: are there any specific **triggers** that seem to come back time and time again?

Example:

Let's go back to the organic shampoo for Latinas. Through customer interviews, the founders discovered that a major **trigger** was the anticipation of a big social event—a birthday, a night out, anything where the women wanted to look and feel their best. This insight moved the founders beyond simply saying, "Our target audience is Latinas," which is bland as fuck, to identify a specific context—the desire to shine at a social event—which adds depth to defining a clear **segment**.

Example:

For the toilet packet company, we've found through online review mining that most customers use it while traveling and/or when they need to share toilets with others. This might sound too simple, but those two situations seem to be tightly linked to their main **segment**.

TAKE ACTION

Understanding *when* your **segment** feels the need for what you offer is as important as understanding *why*.

Here's what to do:

1. **Review your insights.** Look back at the patterns and themes you uncovered about your customers, especially anything related to what motivates them to take action.

2. **Identify common triggers.** What specific events or situations consistently pop up? These are your **triggers**.

3. **Define context.** Combine your understanding of your customers' needs with their triggers. For example, instead of "busy moms," you might have "busy moms overwhelmed with packing school lunches."

List of contextual attributes:

- _____
- _____
- _____
- _____
- _____

Step 3. Find Your RAGE

This method helps you evaluate whether a potential segment is a good fit for your business in the long run. A particular **segment** may look good on paper, but the reality is always more nuanced. To select the right one, I advise scoring each against four key factors.

And because I've noticed that this is a highly emotional process and brings loads of negative feelings—feelings of missing out, fear of committing to anything just in case—I call this the **RAGE** framework (Figure 6.3), which stands for **R**evenue, **A**ccess, **G**rowth, and **E**njoyment.

Figure 6.3. The RAGE framework.

Revenue: *Do they spend a good percentage of their money on the category?*

Prioritize customers who spend a significant portion of their disposable income in your **category**, regardless of their overall income level. Why? Because someone who consistently spends a small amount of money is more valuable than someone who's super rich but rarely (or ever!) spends in that same **category**.

For example, my friend Luke is an amateur birder—he loves to observe wild birds in their natural habitats. He told me he spends around 5 percent of his income on birding every year on things like trips abroad or new equipment. And, more interestingly, he also knows birders with low income who would easily spend 10–20 percent of their income on it.

Beware of those growth-hacking experts who advise you to sell to the wealthy. If you were to cater to birders, a multimillionaire who couldn't care less about wild birds wouldn't be as valuable as a teenager who spends most of her pocket money photographing woodpeckers.

Access: *Do you have access to this segment?*

This is where dreams of standing the f*ck out typically go to die. Say you've found the perfect **segment** . . . but can you *actually* reach the people in that **segment**? Can you pick up the phone and call 50 of them today? Or do you have *zero* clue where to even start?

In other words, planning is easy—anyone can create an 89-page business plan—but selling is hard. If you're starting from scratch with no clue where to find your **segment**, how are you going to make any money?

Growth: *Is this segment bursting with the energy of a Parisian fashion show?*

Is it expanding rapidly, indicating potential for future growth? Stagnating? Shrinking?

One way to get an idea is to tap into your existing knowledge of the market. Again, this is why access is important; if you hang out where your **segment** tends to hang out, you will naturally be able to feel whether the energy is there. Another tip: Follow the trailblazers. Identify a couple of folks in your field who who like to try new things, and who like to talk about it.

Finally, you don't have to rely solely on gut feeling. There are tools[31] to help you gauge whether specific terms or topics are on the rise. But, ultimately, you will never be able to find information that says, "*Oui, oui*, this exact **segment** you're thinking about selecting is growing at a rate of 45.989765469 percent per year!"

Enjoyment: *Does this segment make you happy?*

Forget "target audience"—we're talking about humans here. Humans you actually like. My first job out of uni was at a French car manufacturer's regional command center in Dublin, Ireland. There was a little problem, however: I couldn't care less about cars. By extension, I had a tough time connecting with the dealership owners and employees. It just wasn't my thing. Building a business to serve them would have been a terrible, terrible idea.

In other words, to pick a **segment** you're happy and confident about, to have solid foundations to go the distance, aim to find people who bring you joy.

---

31   Josh Howarth. 2024. "How to Spot Trends Before They Happen." *Exploding Topics.* https:// explodingtopics.com/blog/how-to-spot-trends.

TAKE ACTION

Use the RAGE framework to evaluate potential customer segments.

Here's what to do:

1. **List potential segments.** Write down all the customer groups you could serve using the attributes you've uncovered in steps 1 and 2.

2. **Score each segment (on a scale of 1 to 5).** Rate each segment from 1 (low) to 5 (high) based on the RAGE framework:

   ○ **Revenue.** How much do they spend in your **category**?

   ○ **Access.** Can you easily reach and connect with them?

   ○ **Growth.** Is this **segment** expanding or stagnant?

   ○ **Enjoyment.** Do you genuinely enjoy working with them?

3. **Calculate the total score.** Add up the scores for each **segment**.

4. **Prioritize the high scores.** Focus on **segments** with the highest RAGE scores.

My top-scoring **segment** is: _____

_____

_____

Why I chose this **segment**: _____

The Doubts: "What if I Pick the Wrong Segment?"

"Why can't I pick three, four, or even five different segments?"

It's likely because you're focusing on differences that aren't important. Instead of seeing these groups as separate, try finding what *connects* them. Once you know what they share, you can unite them under one core **segment** and then find different ways to reach them.

"What if I pick the wrong segment?"

Let me guess: You wonder if there's another **segment** you haven't thought about. You might change your mind tomorrow, look back at it, and won't fully commit. And then you'll feel miserable.

Remember, you'll *never* have perfect data. Things will always feel chaotic. So trust your instincts and take a leap of faith, because focusing on a specific group doesn't limit your growth; it's a necessary step to becoming known by **category** buyers and generating revenue to expand later.

"Won't targeting a specific segment limit the potential for growth?"

No; quite the opposite, in fact. By solving **ignored struggles** for a specific **segment** in a way that **alternatives** don't, we increase the chance that the folks in this group will buy from us because we give them a compelling reason to.

Also:

- **I don't think I've ever worked with a business that went too narrow.** Like, ever. It's almost always the opposite (as in going too wide and drowning).

- **Going narrow essentially helps you become the *least risky* option** (which is called "satisficing"[32]) for the people in your **segment** since you're the *only* one who can solve their **struggles** in that **category**.

- **People know that niche things are often better.** (You're not going to call a handyman to fix an industrial plumbing system.)

- **You avoid competing directly against too many businesses.** Instead, you can build partnerships—which is vital if you run a small business.

- **And your segment can (and should!) evolve.** Once you generate enough money and interest in that space, you can expand to more customers who fit your criteria or adjacent markets. For example, the Jacuzzi brothers initially designed their hydrotherapy pump to

---

32 A portmanteau of *satisfy* and *suffice*, coined by economist Herbert A. Simon, describes how people search for alternatives until a threshold is met. "Satisficing." Wikipedia. https://en.wikipedia.org/wiki/Satisficing

alleviate the pain of a family member with rheumatoid arthritis. They then expanded to the healthcare and luxury markets.

Let's say you do pick a **segment** that's too narrow . . . what's the *worst* thing that could happen?

You'll notice it quickly (there won't be any customers or not enough). Then you'll learn from it and adjust course. And then you'll have taken action instead of just thinking about your niche for the next 20 months without doing anything about it.

In other words, the very act of focusing our attention is what gives us a distinct advantage and the ability to grow. Focusing on a specific **segment** is a strategic move, not a permanent limitation.

"Won't I get bored focusing on just one segment?"

I'm going to let my friend Nikita Morell, a copywriter who *only* works with architects,[33] answer this one:

"People always ask me if I get bored working with only architects—but my answer is that every architecture firm is unique in its own way . . . I only get to know the industry deeper and deeper, which means I'm becoming more and more of an expert every day."

In other words, focusing doesn't shrink your brain—it expands it! When you obsess over one group of people, you'll discover new ways to connect, learn, and grow, every single day.

Now, I know what you're thinking: *But I'm multi-potential, I have so many interests!* Great news, you can channel those passions—as shown in Figure 6.4—to solve problems in ways that no one else can replicate. Your diverse background isn't going to waste; it's fueling your creativity.

---

33 Check out Nikita's work here: https://nikitamorell.com/.

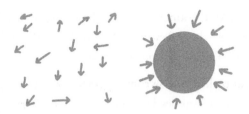

Figure 6.4. Channel your interests toward the same goal.

"Doesn't Byron Sharp say differentiation is useless?"

That's true. In *How Brands Grow*, Sharp says that pretending a brand is different (*perceived* differentiation) doesn't make people want to buy from you. However, *meaningful* differentiation—solving ignored **struggles** for a specific **segment** in a way that **alternatives** don't—does make people more likely to buy from you.

As businesses grow, *meaningful* differentiation becomes harder to achieve, which is why big brands focus on being distinctive instead (we'll cover this in Stage 3).

The Recap: Marketing Consultant for Left-Handed Chiropractors

We're not meant to suffocate in a box labeled "Marketing Consultant for Left-Handed Chiropractors Who Treat Only Dachshunds." Instead, we've learned to obsess over a specific **segment**—a group of people you can serve in a way that gives you a distinct advantage, like Orelsan rapping about the struggles of young French people living in the suburbs.

Let's recap the key takeaways from this chapter:

- **Forget restrictive niching.** Ditch the pressure of narrow industry or demographic boxes. Instead, focus on a specific group of people whose shared struggles you can solve better than anyone else.

- **Describe your segment concisely.** Keep it simple and focused on the shared struggles and context that make this group unique.

- **Use the RAGE framework to evaluate segments.** Score potential segments based on **Revenue, Access, Growth,** and **Enjoyment** to find the perfect fit for your business.

- **Don't fear picking the "wrong" segment.** Trust your gut, take action, and adjust course as needed. Remember, focusing on a specific group doesn't limit your growth; it fuels it.

7

The Category

Back in 2015, I had saved up $20,000 to start my own business—or so I thought. I had this idea for an online tool that would help online stores send emails to customers based on their actions. I spent months daydreaming about being a start-up founder, but I was more like a mime stuck in an invisible box.

This software product lived only in my mind. Not a single line of code was ever written for it. I was busy being busy instead of working on what really mattered: gauging demand, selling something to customers and building a first version.

My savings account was hemorrhaging money faster than I could earn it. My girlfriend at the time (who's now my wife, bless her) gave me an ultimatum: "Listen, you're going to have to make some money because this is fucking stupid." It was a good wake-up call because it *was* fucking stupid.

So I dropped the idea of becoming the next Zuckerberg (see Figure 7.1) and pivoted to selling my time by offering marketing services. I made a spreadsheet of all my contacts, from uncles to ex-colleagues, and contacted them one by one to get some referrals. My aim was to help businesses improve their websites so that they sold more (this is called conversion rate optimization, or CRO).

Figure 7.1. Louis standing awkwardly and dying inside.

The businesses in Dublin, where I've been for the last 14 years, clearly needed to make more money online. I thought I was on to something since no one else was doing it locally.

I managed to consult for a few small companies and some big ones (including tech companies like Dropbox and Phorest) and even had a team of three working with me from Spain and the United States. But it felt like I was trying to pedal a bicycle uphill with a baguette for a wheel. See Figure 7.2 to really understand what this experience was like.

Figure 7.2. Cycling is hard when you use baguettes instead of wheels.

Yes, I was getting some traction, but at what cost? After 18 months, I found myself mentally drained, spending most of my time glued to my laptop, endlessly checking email and Twitter. And I fucking hated the very job I had created for myself.

Around the same time, I got the opportunity to work for Hotjar—a company I admired for its transparency[34]—and I just knew I had to take a break from consulting and close the agency.

The Problem: One Does Not Simply Create Demand

It took me a while to understand why I struggled so much. Turns out, I was like a chef trying to convince Irish tourists to try snails with garlic-herb butter when all they wanted was lasagna. **I was trying to *create* demand for services that the people in my segment (1) didn't know about and (2) didn't feel like they needed.**

It never occurred to me that, maybe, just maybe, there were few (if any) others doing this because conversion rate optimization services were *not* in demand in Dublin. In fact, all the other agencies I knew about focused on ads, social media management, and search engine optimization.

There was a market force that was completely out of my control: category demand. How do you avoid making the same mistake I made?

The Solution: Be Where the Demand Is

You can't create demand for anything because demand is too large for you to create. The demand has to be out there.

— EUGENE SCHWARTZ

A category is a label for a group of similar products or services aimed at a similar audience. It helps people quickly understand what something is.

---

34   See how transparent Hotjar's founder David Darmanin was when he started the company. 2015. "The Hotjar Story (Part 1)—from Idea to 60,000 Beta Signups in 6 Months." *Hotjar.* https://www. hotjar.com/blog /the-hotjar-story-part-1- from-idea-to-60000-beta-signups-in-6-months/.

And there's no official rulebook for **categories**. They're fluid and constantly evolving based on how people use them. For example, some words change meaning, like "computer" (initially referred to people who computed calculations and now means electronic devices); some disappear, like "Walkman" (used to be synonymous with a portable audio player); and new ones emerge constantly, like "influencer" . . . And we cannot do anything about it.

> **It's humbling to realize that we, people doing marketing, have very *little* control over the will of the people we seek to serve.** Just like you can't make a tornado with a $35 desk fan you bought after coming across a post on Instagram, you can't create demand. This is one of the hard lessons the bro marketers don't tell you—and the cause of a lot of frustration for the people I help.

This means that your goal is to position in a **category** that's in demand and that your **segment** both understands and wants. This exercise is helpful to:

1. **Make it easy to compare.** We don't like making decisions from scratch, because it's tiring. That's why it's important to put what you sell in a group that's easy to compare with others. This way, customers can make choices more easily.[35]

2. **Stick to what people already know.** People don't like taking risks or trying things they don't know, so getting them to try a brand-new thing they've never heard of can be really hard. You usually have to start with a few risk-takers or early adopters crossing the chasm before others join in (and this can take years).

3. **Provide mental relief.** Our brains hate chaos. We try to find patterns and meanings in things, even if they don't have any. By positioning correctly, you can help people avoid confusion and make it easier for them to choose what you're selling.

---

35 This is the concept of relativity as discussed in Dan Ariely's book, *Predictably Irrational: The Hidden Forces That Shape Our Decisions.* HarperCollins, 2010.

In other words: *if I fits, I sits.*

The Plan: Four Steps to Take to Find Your Category

There is no greater impediment to the advancement of knowledge than the ambiguity of words.

— THOMAS REID

Your goal is to position your area of focus in a **category** (1) that's in demand and (2) that your **segment** understands. **This means that we must avoid ambiguity at all costs: the words we use to describe the category must be as clear as possible.**

Step 1. Find Your Unique Strengths

This technique helps you find good-fit categories for your product or service by focusing on its unique strengths—instead of slapping lipstick on a pig. It's about highlighting what you're uniquely positioned to do so the right customers choose you over others.

For example, if an animal has a long neck, eats leaves from tall trees, has patchy brown spots, and has extremely long legs, it *has* to be a giraffe. In this example, the **category** is the giraffe, without any ambiguity, since no other animals would fit this description.

Now let's up the ante a bit.

If an establishment opens at 7 p.m.; employs improv comedians; offers burgers, wings, and fries to patrons; and is a place where you can bring your entire family for special occasions . . . it has to be an *interactive restaurant* where the servers are part of the show. Or maybe it's a *comedy improv show* that happens to serve microwave food during the intermission.

The same offerings could be defined by two **categories**: *interactive restaurant* or *improv show*. This is why abductive reasoning, as the Queen of Positioning

April Dunford[36] calls it, is a great way to find all possible **categories** in order to find one that might give you a distinct advantage. To use this technique:

- Take the most common and painful **struggles** you've identified.
- For each, describe the features: how they're going to be solved.
- Then come up with possible **categories** that would contain some (or all) of those features.

Example:

Two years ago, I worked with Sam Conniff, the author of *Be More Pirate*, on his new project called *Uncertainty Experts*. He had assembled a team of neuroscientists and Netflix producers to create an *interactive documentary*— the first of its kind. Their goal? To help teams in high-pressure corporate environments become more comfortable with uncertainty and avoid burnout.

But there was a problem. They were not selling to big companies as much as they'd hoped. We discovered that the issue stemmed from the terms they used to describe what they were selling. Their uncertainty tolerance training contained three hours of documentary episodes to watch, so they called it an **interactive documentary.**

Humor me for a sec. **Can you imagine bringing a five-figure invoice for an *interactive documentary* to your VP of finance?** You'd probably be escorted out of the building *manu militari* by two security guards as big as André the Giant. Next thing you know, you'd end up in the middle of the courtyard, lying face down on a worn, wooden platform, ready to get your head chopped by a guillotine restored for the occasion.

Let's use abductive reasoning to find better options.

Remember, Sam was selling primarily to HR directors who wanted to reduce team burnout so the employees could become more creative at solving problems. He went **insight foraging** and unearthed the following **struggles**:

- Make burnout less likely.

---

36 April Dunford is the author of *Obviously Awesome: How to Nail Product Positioning so Customers Get It, Buy It, Love It.* Ambient Press, 2019.

THE CATEGORY | 155

- Help people feel more positive about the company.
- Reduce feelings of being overwhelmed.
- Improve people's ability to handle unexpected situations.

From those, we can infer the types of products/services—the **alternatives**—that typically help HR directors solve those **struggles** for their employees:

- **Mindfulness apps.** Allowing the employees to practice mindfulness from their phones
- **Employee assistance programs (EAPs).** Counseling and support services tailored to each team member
- **Training courses.** Programs delivered by outside experts
- **Team-building events.** Who doesn't like playing mini-golf with colleagues?

Finally, because *Uncertainty Experts* already had a three-hour interactive documentary developed, we decided that training was the best **category** to lean on. To be more specific (and to leave no ambiguity), a *cohort-based training course.*

"Interactive documentary" sounded like a silly expense to HR departments. "Cohort-based training course" resonated better because it aligned with:

- **Budgets.** HR is used to investing in training, not documentaries.
- **The features offered.** The *Uncertainty Experts* team provided much more than a three-hour watching session: a five-hour training program, video lessons, online events, and personal reports for each participant.
- **Expectations.** It conveyed credibility compared with the perceived entertainment value of a documentary.

Within a couple of weeks, the change in language helped them close two new clients.

TAKE ACTION

To use abductive reasoning to find your unique strengths, follow these steps:

1. **Take the ignored struggles you've identified in Chapter 5.**

2. **Explore potential categories.** Based on the **struggles** you address, brainstorm a list of potential **categories** your offering could fit into. What or who typically solves them? What specific words are used to describe what this is without any ambiguity?

3. **Zero in on the categories** that would put your area of focus in the best light possible to have the best chance of winning as an underdog.

My potential **categories**:

- _____
- _____
- _____

Step 2. Hop in the Trojan Horse

This method consists of presenting what you do in a way that aligns with the segment's current understanding/expectations of the market. It's super helpful when you can describe in great detail what you do and for whom, but *really* struggle to put a label on it.

You don't feel comfortable with any existing **category** because it's not exactly what you do, and it tends to have a bad rep. As a result, you avoid using terms that your **segment** typically understands and wants and resort to creating your own **category** that no one fucking understands.

You'd use a well-established **category** as your Trojan horse, and then, once you have your people's attention, you introduce them to a more unique/complex offering: the soldiers hidden inside the giant wooden horse.

Put differently, the giant horse is what the **segment** *thinks* is needed (a **category** in demand), and the Greek soldiers are what the **segment** *really* needs (your own thing that might not be very well understood).

Here's the catch: it's better to pick a category that is in demand and understood with an 80 percent match to what you do than create something that feels like a 100 percent match that no one fucking understands or wants.

Example:

I met Florian M. Heinrichs,[37] a German-based marketing consultant, through LinkedIn a couple of years ago. He's the kind of no-nonsense marketer I like to hang out with virtually. He got in touch because his business was doing really well (he's booked out for most of the year), but something was bugging him.

You see, he helps mid-sized (25 employees or more) management consulting firms prepare for exits or just grow more, but he felt like something wasn't clicking when sharing his expertise. "Everything I could ever say about marketing has been said a million times," he told me.

He hired me to help him out. First, I asked about his *best* clients (just like when we channeled our best customers back in Chapter 2). He told me he most enjoyed working with (1) the up-and-comer firm principals who were about to take over and wanted to grow and (2) the older generation looking to sell their firms who are horrified by the lowball offers they're getting from potential buyers.

Both have something in common, though.

They have "two business degrees and a doctorate" (read: "highly educated"), and they're very good at selling to their network—aka business development. **But marketing? Oh, marketing is like a dirty word: "Why the fuck do we**

---

37   You can find Florian's LinkedIn profile here: https://www.linkedin.com/in/fmheinrichs/.

need marketing? To make our business cards pretty?" They think it's a waste of time.

(*Obvious note:* Of course, that's not really what marketing is. But that's how the firm's principals see it.)

Florian was positioning his services as a *professional services* **marketing** *consultancy*. The problem became very obvious to both of us. How are you supposed to share your *marketing* expertise with folks who think it's a waste of time?

At the end of our first call, he had two choices: keep fighting against it or adapt using the Trojan horse method. He could continue expending energy to convince people that business development was essentially marketing, draining his resources as a solopreneur. Or he could adapt his language to align with their understanding, making sales without the need to educate or burn out.

We talked again two weeks later.

"So . . . ," Florian said, "the business development versus marketing thing. That's a win already."

"What do you mean?" I asked.

"I spoke to a couple of people who came inbound. I just flat-out asked a bit of a cheeky question. I asked, 'Are you asking me for help with business development, or is this more of a marketing job?' and they replied, 'Absolutely business development. Dude, we hate marketing.'"

This single change in language made everything click for Florian. By changing just one word—from "marketing" to "biz dev"—in the way he was describing his services to prospects, he gave them what they thought they wanted (business development, not marketing). And then, once he got their attention, he introduced them to a more nuanced approach that blends business development with proper marketing (what's hidden inside the giant wooden horse). Win-win.

TAKE ACTION

Here's how to use the Trojan horse method to bridge the gap between what people think they need and what they really need:

1. **Identify potential Trojan horses.** What established **categories** resonate with your ideal clients, even if it's not a perfect fit? What do they *think* they need?

2. **Talk to your peeps.** Which of those Trojan horses do they connect with the most? Which ones do they roll their eyes at?

3. **Select the best match.** Remember, an 80 percent match with a familiar term is better than a 100 percent match with a confusing one.

My potential Trojan horse **categories** are:

- _____
- _____
- _____

Step 3. Sprinkle Some Extra Clarity

This method involves enhancing an existing category with carefully chosen details—qualifiers—for added clarity. The people in your **segment** already have groups of products/services established in their minds. Instead of inventing new terms that would confuse them, we use established **categories** to lean on and add details that shine a light on what we do best. It's yet another way to communicate very clearly why you're the shit.

Take the air fryer, first developed by the French company SEB, as an example. It does not use as much oil as other fryers (40 percent fewer calories and 80 percent less fat, to be exact), but—and this is important—it's still a fryer.

- **Small category.** Air fryer

- **Broader category.** Fryer
- **General category.** Small cooking appliances
- **Even more general category.** Kitchen appliances

SEB did *not* claim to have invented a whole new appliance category with the air fryer. The company took something people already knew—a fryer—and added a special twist: cooking with *air* instead of *oil*. Customers instantly understand what the appliance does (it's still a fryer!), but the "air" part highlights a major benefit: *healthier* frying.

You can add three types of qualifiers to an existing **category**, as shown in Table 7.1.

Table 7.1. The Three Types of Qualifiers

Pairing	Description	Examples
Category + Segment	An existing **category** paired with a key **segment** attribute	• Organic shampoo **(category)** for Latinas **(segment)** • Breed-specific **(segment)** dog chew treat **(category)**
Category + Struggle	An existing **category** paired with a solution to a frustrating **struggle**	• Breathable **(struggle)** sneakers **(category)** • Air **(struggle)** fryer **(category)**
Category + Category	This one's quite rare, but it combines two existing **categories** to add specificity	• Motel (motor + hotel) • Sitcom (situation + comedy)

These pairings don't mean inventing a whole new **category**. Instead, they bring another level of detail to how your audience already sees a group of products or services.

TAKE ACTION

Don't reinvent the wheel, *s'il vous plaît*. Instead, just add a layer of clarity to an existing **category**. Here's how to do it:

1. **Identify potential categories as your base.** Which established group of products/services does your offering naturally belong to? (Think "fryer," not "air fryer," initially).

2. **Play with different qualifiers.** What would happen if you were to append a quick way to describe your **segment**? A brief description of an **ignored struggle** you solve well?

3. **Talk to your peeps.** Which of those do they connect with the most? Which ones do they roll their eyes at?

My potential categories **with qualifiers** are:

- _____

- _____

- _____

Step 4. Identify the Best Category

By now you should have a list of potential **categories** for your area of focus. Now you need to pick one. There are two main things to consider, as shown in Table 7.2.

Table 7.2. Criteria to Identify the Best Category

Criteria	Description	What to Look For
Demand	Is there a growing market for this **category**? Are people actively spending money on solutions within it?	Market research data indicating growth trends Evidence of customer spending (e.g., sales figures, industry reports) Presence of competitors and their market share
Secret sauce	What's the secret sauce that you can bring to this **category**?	Exclusive partnerships, solid distribution networks, intellectual property, or a trusted brand name

First, and most important, is demand. Is this a busy market or is it a ghost town? You want a **category** that's *in demand*. Think of it like surfing—you want to be on the wave as it's forming, not as it's fizzling out.

My first real marketing job was at an Irish start-up selling bulk SMS solutions to local shops like butchers or beauty salons—they'd use our tool to send text messages with coupons to their existing customers. It was an easy sale for those already sold on the power of SMS, even if it often boiled down to a price war with competitors. But convincing anyone else? Those who weren't already using SMS marketing? It was as easy as force-feeding escargot to Americans. Prospects were more interested in building mobile apps or pouring more money into social media ads. You could just feel that the energy in the bulk SMS **category** wasn't there.

My best tip to spot a category that's in demand is to follow the trailblazers, the ones who seem to be living in the future. They're often the first to talk about the next big things. But don't chase trends just because they're shiny. Look for *real* momentum.

The second thing to consider is your secret sauce. Can you solve your chosen **segment's struggles** in a way that others can't? Do you have unique tech, a trusted brand, or a partnership that gives you an edge?

In summary, choose a **category** with genuine demand and one where you can leverage your unique strengths to solve specific **struggles** effectively.

TAKE ACTION

Choosing the right category is like picking the perfect wave to surf—you want momentum and a unique style.

Here's what to do:

1. **Analyze demand.** From your list of potential categories, identify those with a growing market. Look for:

   ○ Market research data showing growth trends

   ○ Evidence of customer spending (sales figures, industry reports)

   ○ Presence of competitors and their market share

2. **Identify your secret sauce.** For each **category** with high demand, pinpoint your unique advantage:

   ○ Exclusive partnerships?

   ○ Solid distribution networks?

   ○ Intellectual property?

   ○ Trusted brand name?

3. **Choose your wave.** Select the **category** with strong demand where you can leverage your secret sauce to solve your target **segment's struggles** better than anyone else.

My **category** with high demand and my unique advantage is:

_____

The Doubts: "But I Want Zero Competition!"

"How can I find ignored struggles in a category that already exists?"

It seems to be a contradiction, like searching for a buried treasure on an island that's been fully explored.

On one hand, we want to find unique **struggles** that others ignore. On the other, we need to place ourselves in an existing **category**, taking advantage of the established market dynamics. Alex M H Smith[38] calls this approach "weirding the normal," where the "normal" is the existing **category** and the "weirding" is the unique way you address some of the specific **struggles**.

You're essentially using a metal detector on an island that's been combed over with regular detectors for years. You're not exploring new territory, but you're using a new approach to uncover hidden treasures everyone else has missed.

*"I'm afraid of crowded markets! How can I stand the f*ck out?"*

Look, I get it. We all dream of a market with *zero* competition and *endless* customers. But in reality, a market full of competitors (both direct and indirect) is a good thing. It means there's real demand, a hunger for what's being offered.

This means it presents a significant opportunity. You can tap into existing demand, build on what people already know, and challenge the status quo to stand the f*ck out.

"But I want to do something completely new!"

"Nothing is lost, nothing is created, all things are merely transformed." That's from Antoine Lavoisier, a renowned French chemist. You can't create something new; you can just use things that have already been used before and combine them in new ways. You might feel like an impostor because you didn't come up with ideas yourself. A creative thief, if you will.

---

38 Alex M H Smith. *No Bullsh*t Strategy*. Troubador Publishing, 2023.

Your opportunity here is that, by focusing so much on specific **struggles** in specific **segments** and playing inside specific **categories**, you can really find ways things *haven't* been done inside something that *has* been done.

"I hate the category we're supposed to be in. What should I do?"

As a famous emperor once said, "Let the hate flow through you!"

Essentially, choose the **category** that *logically* fits your **segment** best even if it's not your favorite. Instead of letting that dislike hold you back, use it as fuel to challenge the norms and shake things up.

"I don't want to be a _____."

This comment usually comes from solopreneurs or small business owners. You may not want to call yourself a "marketing coach" or a "stock trader" because you don't want to associate who you are with the **category** you're in. But don't get too hung up on labels.

A couple of years ago, I was advising a Belgium-based customer experience (CX) consultant who wanted to shake things up in her business. At the time, she was offering career coaching services for CX folks, but she didn't want to call herself a coach. It had negative connotations for her—folks with no skin in the game, no real diploma, no experience, just telling others what to do—but she eventually gave it a go after looking at the evidence: career coaching was in demand, and she could take advantage of it. She still offers coaching, and now her expertise speaks louder than any preconceived label.

The Recap: Selling Snails to Irish Tourists

Don't try to sell snails with garlic-herb butter to Irish tourists who just want lasagna. That was me, trying to create demand for something nobody wanted. In this chapter, we've learned that demand is a force of nature, not a growth-hacking campaign.

Let's recap the key takeaways from this chapter:

- **Zero competition might mean zero demand.** Find a **category** that's buzzing, not one you have to resuscitate.

- **Three ways to sniff out your category:**
  - ○ **Unique strengths.** Find what you do best.
  - ○ **Trojan horse.** Sneak your brilliance inside something familiar. If people think they need a "business development" guy, be the "business development" guy who secretly sprinkles in marketing magic.
  - ○ **Qualifiers.** Don't be afraid to tweak existing **categories**. An "air fryer" is still a fryer, just . . . better.

- **Pick a category that's hot, but where you can also bring something unique to the table.** Think partnerships, tech, or a brand people trust.

- **Don't fear the crowded market.** Competition means there's gold to be mined.

The Recap: Unique Positioning

Unique positioning *isn't* about being different just to be different—it's about finding a meaningful difference by solving overlooked problems for a specific group of people and doing it better than anyone else. In this stage, we used the juicy insights uncovered in Stage 1 to identify **job, alternatives, struggles, segment,** and **category,** summed up in Figure S2.3, reproduced here from the introduction to Stage 2.

Figure S2.3. The five core insights of unique positioning.

Let's recap the key takeaways from this stage:

- **The job is the specific, timeless goal your segment wants to achieve,** such as "mask bathroom odors." It's the anchor we use to find the rest of the insights.

- **Go beyond direct competitors with alternatives.** What other solutions, work-arounds, or DIY approaches are people using to get the job done?

- **Forget logic to tap into the irrational struggles.** Your customers are not rational, and neither are you.

- **Find ignored struggles.** Discover frustrating problems your **alternatives** have overlooked.

- **Obsess over your segment**—a group of people you can serve in a way that gives you a distinct advantage, instead of suffocating in a super-restrictive niche.

- **Pick a hot category, because demand is out of our control.** Don't be afraid of a crowded market.

To wrap things up, let's create a statement that describes your meaningful difference and **unique positioning**.

UNIQUE POSITIONING STATEMENT

Unlike **alternative(s)**, [*area of focus*] is the only **category** to solve **ignored struggle(s)** and get **job** done for **segment**.

For LatinUs Beauty:

Unlike **straightening treatments, two-hour hair routines, or generic shampoos, LatinUs Beauty** is the only **organic shampoo** to **get rid of uncontrollable frizz caused by warm, humid weather** and **get salon-quality, frizz-free hair** made for **Latinas with long, frizzy hair.**

For the PTDC:

Unlike **just working more or selling out for quick cash**, the **PTDC** is the only **online fitness training program** that helps you **overcome self-doubt, build a real business, and create a successful career you love** as a **jacked nerd**—a dedicated trainer who wants to make a difference and is in it for the long haul.

I always tell my clients that this statement is not meant to be seen by customers; it's a tool to give you and/or the people involved *clarity*. So make it as long as you want, and don't worry if it sounds awkward—it's not meant to become your next homepage headline.

Next, let's develop a **distinctive brand**.

Distinctive Brand

Back when I was a cheeky 15-year-old, I had this weird obsession with contradicting people (*quelle surprise*, right?). Teachers, friends, family—nobody was safe. I was desperate for attention, and playing the devil's advocate was my go-to move.

One day, during history class, I landed a particularly clever remark that earned some laughs from my classmates. My teacher, however, wasn't amused. His face turned beet-red as he yelled, "Louis, why can't you stay quiet? I can't get through any of my classes without you interrupting us every five minutes!" Followed by: "You're an intellectual terrorist!"

Loud gasp

That *really* bothered me.

I wanted to be seen, of course, but I also really, really, *really* needed people to like me. And it was clear from my teacher's remark that my approach wasn't working. Shouting random opinions was getting people's attention, but at what cost? I was getting noticed at the expense of trust.

Most of my teachers didn't enjoy my presence in the classroom, and most of my classmates were getting increasingly irritated by my antics—so much so that when I ran for class representative, expecting an easy win, I lost by a landslide to my best friend. *Fucking ouch!*

I learned there's a fine line between being *disruptive* and being *distinctive*. *Disruption* gets attention for all the wrong reasons at the expense of trust. Being *distinctive*, on the other hand, allows you to stand the f*ck out *without* alienating others or sacrificing relationships.

Today, I'm still a natural contrarian, of course, but I've learned to channel it better. And that's what we'll explore in this next stage: developing a **distinctive brand** that helps you stand the f*ck out for all the right reasons, *without* alienating your audience.

In this stage you will uncover four additional elements: **monster, point of view (POV), spices,** and **assets.** (See Figure S3.1.)

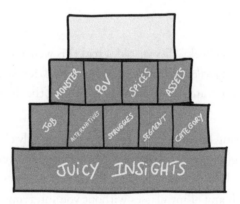

Figure S3.1. The four additional insights used to craft a distinctive brand.

You'll use those new elements to create a **one-page distinctive brand kit** that contains everything your brand needs to turn heads.

8

The Monster

The first step to building a **distinctive brand** that does *not* drive people away is to unite them against a common enemy or obstacle—instead of making it all about you.

A story:

It's match day in Danbury, Connecticut; a quiet, unassuming town 50 kilometers from New York City.

More than 3,000 roaring fans are lining up in front of the Danbury Ice Arena to watch their local team—the Trashers—play a low-level minor professional ice hockey (UHL) game. Even pro wrestler John Cena is in attendance. And it's sold out, once again.

Now, 3,000 people may not seem like a lot, but the town of Danbury has never had that many hockey fans attend an entire season, let alone one game.

So how did that happen?

Enter James Galante, the founder of the East Coast's largest garbage collection company. He paid half a million dollars for the right to build a team and then handed the reins to his 17-year-old son, A.J.

Yup, you read that right. 17.

"The Trashers are what I love in one big freaking mix of things: pro wrestling and The Mighty Ducks combined." A.J. explained. "We want that bad boy image. We wanted to be the home for that 1 percent that cheered for the bad guys."[39]

They didn't just talk the talk. No, no; they *were* bad guys.

They would routinely turn off the hot water in the other team's locker room. They'd drop their gloves and fight the second the ref started the game (setting a league record for penalty minutes). The fans in the stadium would bring body bags and throw them on the ice whenever a rival player got knocked out.

They had a **distinctive brand**. And everyone loved it.

Well, not *everyone*.

The Problem: Are You Blaming the Wrong People?

The UHL commissioner *hated* the Danbury Trashers. He saw their antics as an embarrassment to the league, a stain on the noble sport of hockey. **For him, playing *proper* hockey was more important than entertaining the fans.**

The Trashers could have easily caved to the commissioner's pressure. They could have agreed that winning was everything and that fans should just get on board with the league's vision. But blaming the fans for wanting a different kind of hockey would have been a big mistake. *Huuuuge!*

- It would've been a slap in the face to their diehard fans, who would feel betrayed.
- It would have made the team blend the f*ck in with the league.
- It probably would have been a one-way ticket to financial ruin.

39 Chapan Way and Maclain Way, executive producers. 2021. *Untold: Crimes and Penalties.* Featuring A.J. Galante, James Galante, and Richard Brosal. Netflix. https://www.imdb.com/title/tt15101956/.

The Galantes had to decide what mattered more: pleasing the league while blaming their fanbase, or doubling down on what made them distinctive.

The Solution: Rally People Around You

They chose the second option, of course.

They were clever enough to use the clash with the UHL commissioner to their advantage. They rallied their fans around them, saying, "It's not your fault you find hockey boring; it's the purists who suck the fun out of it." **This finger-pointing gave the people of Danbury something to blame and a reason to show up to their local ice hockey arena every weekend.** The Galantes were taking guilt from their **segment** and redirecting it at the **monster**.

> **The monster is a semi-fictional enemy representing some of the problems the people in your segment face.** By giving a name to their **struggles**, you aim to give them a clear enemy to blame, making their world easier to understand and control. Your brand then becomes the natural way to help them fight it.

I've taught this idea for a while now and people really like it. It helps you talk to the people on your team clearly and get them excited without putting down competitors or doing anything unethical.

First, and this is crucial: the monster you pick must prevent those in your segment from feeling guilty about their struggles and inability to get the job done. In other words, the **monster** is there to deflect the blame to something (or someone else), which provides both relief and a sense of control. This rapport-building gives you a distinct advantage. You'll bypass the typical sales pitch that customers tune out, unlike competitors who struggle to move past, "Here's our product; buy it now, pretty please; we have shareholders to feed."

For example, it's not the Danbury residents' fault if they're bored out of their minds when watching their team play; it's the purists' fault the game got turned into a borefest. See how powerful that is?

Second, the monster you pick must be responsible for some of the problems your segment is facing. It's positioned as the cause of some of the problems faced by the **segment** in a way that stands the test of time. This is yet another way to get people on your side without having to try so hard to win their "loyalty."

For example, for the Danbury Trashers, the hockey purists and their beliefs are the reason why people are bored watching hockey (which is the main **struggle**).

Third, picking the right monster simplifies choices for the people in your segment. It creates a clear-cut scenario: Either they choose you and finally get their job done, or they stick with the status quo and let the **monster** devour them whole. This clarity is a breath of fresh air in a world overflowing with options.

For example, Danbury residents can watch other boring sports or watch the Trashers destroy their opponents every weekend. Table 8.1 shows potential **monster** examples for the Danbury Trashers.

Table 8.1. Evaluating Potential Monsters for Danbury Trashers

Potential Monsters	Evaluation	Comments
The soft hockey fans who prefer finesse over entertainment	Incorrect	Pointing the finger at this group would probably drive a wedge in our **segment**, blaming them for their **struggles**.
The media, who portray hockey as boring	Incorrect	Blaming the media doesn't really explain why the fans are struggling. It's not the cause of their problems.

Potential Monsters	Evaluation	Comments
The other teams in the league, who prefer winning in front of an empty stadium	Incorrect	Blaming the other teams could be seen as a cheap shot.
The purists of the hockey game	**Correct**	Pointing the finger at the purists deflects the blame from the fans and rallies them around a common cause without shitting on other teams.

The Four Types of Monster

The Corporate Giant

This type of monster is a massive, faceless corporation, so obsessed with quarterly profits that it forgets about the people it's supposed to serve. You know, like big oil and gas companies that knew since the 1970s that burning fossil fuels would cause dramatic environmental effects. Yet they chose to keep their research as their dirty little secret and gaslight the public into thinking climate change was junk science.

As another example, LatinUs Beauty's founders started the company because no household hair care brands were designed *specifically* for Latinas. Sure, other products might work for curly or wavy hair, but those big brands didn't understand their unique culture and heritage. LatinUs Beauty is pointing the finger at the corporate giant.

If you're pointing the finger at a big competitor just because it has a huge market share and you're low-key jealous, choosing it as your monster can fall flat—even backfire. However, the corporate giant concept works well if these large entities clearly cause the **struggles** you're solving.

Some examples I've seen in the wild:

- **The Mouse.** Referring to Disney, highlighting its vast media empire and potential monopolistic practices.

- **Big Oil.** Refers to the world's largest publicly traded oil and gas companies, often considered as a collective entity, like ExxonMobil, Chevron, Shell, BP, and TotalEnergies.

- **Big 4.** Referring to the four biggest professional services companies in the world: EY, KPMG, PwC, and Deloitte.

The Alternative Solution

The monster could also be the alternative solution people use to solve their struggles. In this case, we're not pointing the finger at a giant corporation but at the work-arounds, shortcuts, or bundles of solutions that people *have* to use to get the **job** done.

For example, at Hotjar we pointed the finger at "traditional web analytics," exposing the shortcomings of tools that only spit out traffic data—like how many people visited your page and for how long—*without* revealing the human story behind the numbers.

We used this **monster** to (1) let prospects know it wasn't their fault if they couldn't understand what was really happening on their site, (2) show the real source of their problem, and (3) give them a simple choice: continue relying on traditional web analytics alone or add Hotjar to their tool stack to see the human story using website heat maps, anonymized session recordings, or real-time user feedback. (See Figure 8.1.)

Understand how users are really experiencing your site without drowning in numbers

Traditional web analytics tools help you analyze traffic data. But numbers alone can't tell you what users really do on your site — Hotjar will.

Sign up with Google   Sign up with Email

no credit card required

Figure 8.1. Hotjar homepage[40] from 2020.

40   Hotjar. "Hotjar Homepage." 2020. https://web.archive.org/web/20201101000240/https://www.hotjar.com/.

The Culture of the Category

You can also point the finger at beliefs that have stuck in the industry. The big advantage of this type of **monster** is that you don't run the risk of getting backlash because you're not calling anyone out in particular.

Remember how I started this book? I pointed my finger at the toxic growth-hack marketing culture. I highlighted how it's been eroding your confidence, self-worth, and joy in your work, pushing you toward quick fixes sold by so-called experts. **I made it clear it's *not* your fault if you struggle to stand the f*ck out—it's *theirs*.** I also showed I am on your side; I understand your situation because I've lived it. And I presented two simple choices: to continue blending the f*ck in doing things that didn't fulfill you or to stand the f*ck out without selling your soul.

For what it's worth, this is my favorite type of **monster** to use because it has plenty of benefits for very few downsides.

Some examples I've seen in the wild:

- **Hustle culture.** The idea that working crazy long hours at the expense of everything else is required to succeed.
- **Fast fashion.** Cheap, trendy clothes, rapidly produced. It sacrifices ethics and the environment for profit, resulting in worker exploitation, waste, and pollution.

The Monster Within

And finally, the last type of monster could be a feeling, behavior, or something within us that's causing pain. Our brains are wired for survival in a world vastly different from a few centuries/millennia ago, leading to cognitive biases and irrational responses that are not always helpful in the modern world.

For example, *Uncertainty Experts* point the finger at the way humans handle uncertainty, which causes stress, fear, and even burnout. But they do not blame you for it. No. We've evolved over millions of years to fear the unknown. For our ancestors, survival depended on figuring things out quickly. We're just born this way.

When done right, this is a very powerful framing because it helps people deal with deeply ingrained personal **struggles**.

Some notable examples:

- **Fear of missing out (FOMO).** The anxiety of missing out on stuff, fueled by social media.

- **Information overload.** The overwhelming amount of data and content that makes it hard for audiences to focus and make decisions.

The Plan: Create Your Monster

It's time to figure out the specific **monster** you're going to pick for your project. There are three steps you can use to do this.

Step 1. Lean on Your Origin Story

This method involves going back in time to understand why the business was started in the first place in order to infer a monster threatening the segment. We get so caught up in the doing that we forget (or at least take for granted) the reason why the project was started. I've seen this with clients; it's hard to "see the label when you're inside the jar," as David C. Baker puts it.

If you're the founder, the reason why you've built the business might be easy to recall. If you're not, talk to those who started it and longtime employees. They can help you understand the driving force behind the business and what they were fighting for or against. This will help you uncover the **monster** that your business is battling.

Here are some specific prompts to ask.

As a founder:

- *If you could go back to the day before you even created [project name], what was the single biggest frustration you were facing that made you say, "Fuck this, there has to be a better way"?*

- *How has the **monster** we fight evolved since the early days of [project name]?*

For nonfounders:

- *Was there a particular competitor or industry practice that the founders were passionately against? And if so, why?*

- *What would happen if [project name] ceased to exist tomorrow—what would be the consequences for the people we sought to serve?*

For example, when I joined Hotjar, I spoke at length with all five cofounders. I quickly learned that they were all computer nerds[41] who met while working at the same software company. But the juiciest insight came from learning that they started Hotjar to fight against industry best practices that ignored user needs. This **monster** resulted in websites that users found frustrating and difficult to use, ultimately impacting revenue.

You can also look for clues about what the company is fighting for/ against from publicly available content. Are there old blog posts, interviews, and conference keynotes you could unearth to find some hidden gems? Sure, you will probably not find a 20-year-old article titled, "This Is Our **Monster**," but you can infer from what you read what the people in the company were passionate about at the start.

I like to use a website called the Wayback Machine[42]—a digital archive of the internet founded by an American nonprofit—to search for clues in old About pages, press releases, and founder interviews.

For example, this is a bit cringeworthy, but this was the copy I wrote for my agency in 2015. Can you figure out the **monster** I was trying to slay?

Are you on the Light Side of Marketing?

We believe that companies that stand out from the crowd share a common set of attributes. We call it the Light Side of Marketing.

We stand behind those attributes every single day. This is what we believe in. This is our manifesto.

---

41 I say this with the utmost affection.

42 The Wayback Machine is an initiative of the Internet Archive, a 501(c)(3) nonprofit, building a digital library of internet sites and other cultural artifacts in digital form. For more information, go to https://archive.org/about/.

Companies on the Light Side of Marketing share a set of six attributes.

#1: Inner-directed

Those companies have a personality and believe in causes that encourage people to follow and buy from.

#2: Customer-centric

Their products or services, their customer service department, or even the way they treat their employees are all part of their marketing strategy.

#3: Transparent

Transparency breeds trust, and trust breeds loyalty. The transparency movement is a great example of this practice.

#4: Experience-centric

They treat customers as individuals with emotions and feelings and understand both the rational and emotional aspects of the customer journey.

#5: Engaging

Companies on the Light Side of Marketing find ways to talk to their customers, at scale, and engage their audience.

#6: Helpful

Producing truly helpful content is at the top of their agenda, which attracts and retains a clearly-defined audience.

TAKE ACTION

Ask yourself, *What sparked this whole thing? What problem was so frustrating that someone had to fix it?*

If you're not the project's founder, contact the founders. Ask about their origin story and get them to go deep. Record the conversation if you can.

Origin story:

_____

_____

_____

_____

Then listen to the conversation again and try to see if you can spot specific monsters being mentioned along the way:

- ° The corporate giant
- ° The alternative solution
- ° The culture of the **category**
- ° The **monster** within

1. **Fire up the time machine.** Access archived versions of your website, specifically looking at old About pages, press releases, blog posts, and founder interviews.

2. **Read between the lines.** Don't just skim-read. Pay close attention to the way problems and frustrations are mentioned.

3. **Come up with potential monsters.** Corporate giants? **Alternative** solutions? **Category** culture? The **monster** within?

Step 2. Find Out Who's Responsible for Your Segment's Pain

This technique works by identifying the root cause of a struggle your segment is facing in order to unearth its monster. I use it often to prevent the people I advise from getting stuck in a cycle of blaming their **segment** for the issues they're facing.

Similar to the 5 Whys method used in Toyota's lean methodology, it uncovers the root cause of a specific struggle, revealing the true **monster** your audience faces.

Example:

Let's go back to the Hotjar example to illustrate this concept. I'm going to start with a specific **struggle** that Hotjar's **segment** was facing and drill down until I find a potential **monster** to slay.

- **Problem.** We don't know why website conversion rates have dropped.
- **OK, but why?** We don't know which parts of the user journey are causing people to abandon their purchases.
- *D'accord . . .* **why?** We haven't been collecting enough data on user behavior on our website.
- **Why?** Our current analytics tools are limited and don't provide deep enough insights into user interactions.

There we have it. The root cause of their **struggle**. The right **monster** to blame.

Example:

And now let's use one of the biggest **struggles** faced by people like us—the lack of confidence in our work that makes us blend the f*ck in:

- **Problem.** Marketers struggle to stand the f*ck out and feel confident in their work.
- **OK, but why?** They feel pressured to chase quick fixes.
- **D'accord . . . why?** Everywhere they look, someone is promising a "magic trick" to get tons of customers fast.

- **Why?** These "shortcuts" are tempting because standing the f*ck out for real takes time and effort.

- **Ah, OK . . .** but why? The "get-rich-quick" hype makes it seem like slow and steady is for losers and everyone else is getting ahead with tricks.

In this case, it's clear that the **monster** can be a symbol of the get-rich-quick marketing hype.

TAKE ACTION

Let's play detective and uncover the root cause of the struggles holding your customers back in order to identify potential monsters. Here's what to do:

1. **Choose a struggle.** Take a specific **ignored struggle** you've identified in Stage 2.

2. **Channel your inner detective.** Ask "Why?" repeatedly, digging deeper each time to understand the reasons behind the **struggle**. Don't stop until you can no longer go further.

3. **Unmask the monster.** The final "Why?" should reveal the root cause—the true **monster** responsible for your customer's **struggles**—without blaming the customer for it.

Ignored struggle:

Why? _____

_____

Why? _____

_____

Why? _____

_____

Potential **monsters** you want to slay:

- _____

- _____

- _____

Step 3. Pick the Perfect Monster

At this stage, you probably have a bunch of monsters on your list to choose from. Instead of trying to commit to one straight away, start by using some **monster** statements in sales calls, website copy, emails, and one-on-

one conversations—and pay attention to how people react. Do they think you've lost the plot? Or do they understand it immediately?

There's nothing quite as rewarding as hearing people connect with you on a deep, personal level. When they tell you they've felt the same way but couldn't articulate it, it validates all the effort you've poured into applying the concept of this book. It makes all this hard work worthwhile, I promise you.

A few tips:

- **Embrace the obvious.** Don't overthink it. The most effective **monsters** are often staring you right in the face.

- **Keep it simple.** Choose a name that is easy to understand, pronounce, and remember. Your **segment** should understand it easily.

- **Give it time.** Finding the right villain to slay might take a few rounds. So please don't give up. Keep on keepin' on.

Remember, this process might feel weird at first. But once you've said it a few times and heard it echoed back to you, it'll become second nature.

TAKE ACTION

A memorable **monster** will rally the right people around you.

Here's what to do:

1. **Test-drive your monsters.** Insert your **monster** statements into sales calls, website copy, emails, and conversations.

2. **Listen closely.** Pay attention to how people react. Do they connect with your **monster** or seem confused?

3. **Keep it simple.** Choose a name that's easy to understand and remember.

The **monster** that is threatening my **segment** and causing them struggles is: _____

The Doubts: "What if I Annoy People?"

"I'm afraid of pissing people off!"

First, you *don't* have to shout about the **monster** from the rooftops. You can use it internally to guide you. That's what happens with most of the business owners I advise. They rarely call the **monster** out directly on the homepage of their website, for example.

Also, the right **monster** isn't someone or something in particular; it's more like something big and annoying that doesn't care if you call it out. For example, who's going to come knocking at your door if you point the finger at the speed of change in marketing? That's right—no one.

And then, remember, you're not being mean, or pissing people off for the sake of it, or blaming others for fun. You do this to help a specific group of people by standing up against what causes them problems.

"What if the monster one day just disappears? Do you move on to another monster?"

The exercise of identifying the right **monster** is intentionally built to help you and your brand stand the test of time. That's why the four types of **monsters** I've laid out for you tend to be big, intangible things that are unlikely to change from one day to another.

"What if a competitor has the same monster?

You may think that just because you have the same **monster**, you have to slay it the same way, but that's not the case.

First, it will be extremely rare for brands to approach things this way. Second, businesses are unlikely to be savvy enough to use **monsters** the right way. Third, if they do, they're probably not going to talk about it in the exact same way.

In other words, it's *impossible* for others to arrive at the same place.

The Recap: The Art of Finger-Pointing

Don't blame the people in your **segment** for wanting something different. Instead, unite them against a common enemy—a **monster**. This chapter showed you how to pinpoint that **monster** and rally your audience against it.

Let's recap the key takeaways:

- **Don't blame your audience for their struggles.** Instead, identify the real **monster** holding them back. This could be a corporate giant, an alternative solution, the **category's** culture, or even a feeling.

- **Frame your brand as the solution to fight the monster.** This positions you as an ally and gives people a compelling reason to choose you.

- **Use your origin story and customer struggles to identify potential monsters.** Dig deep to understand the root cause of your audience's pain points.

- **Test your monster statements in the wild.** Pay attention to how people react and refine your approach accordingly.

- **Don't overthink it!** The most effective **monsters** are often the most obvious.

9

The Point of View

Now that you have identified the common enemy to deflect the blame to, you've got to find a way to talk about it so it connects with people. But let me guess: You do not want to do it in an "intellectual terrorist" way. You don't want to come across as preachy. And you really, really, *really* don't want to alienate potential customers.

The Problem: Are You Just Shouting Random Opinions?

It's one of the biggest roadblocks keeping brands from genuinely standing the f*ck out: they believe sharing their thoughts means being super divisive, behaving like the intellectual terrorist I once was. They think they have to shout random, even hurtful opinions into the void to be noticed.

They're like little hermit crabs that stay in the comfort of their shell where everything is safe and peaceful. But here's the thing: you can't stay in your shell *and* stand the f*ck out. You're going to have to get noticed one way or another if you want your brand to exist.

By trying to appeal to everyone, you might end up with crickets. Your message gets lost in a sea of *meh*, leaving people scratching their heads.

Without a clear **point of view (POV)**, your actions lack coherence. You're sending mixed signals, leaving people wondering what you stand for and why they should care. They sense this lack of clarity and tune you out.

The Solution: Send the Right Signal

You want to send a clear signal to your people—your segment—that you're there to *protect* them. To help them slay the **monster**. Not just shout random opinions into the void.

A point of view is a collection of consistent messages inserted into everything you do and say, showing the people in your segment you're committed to protecting them and earning their trust. This creates a sense of coherence and control, which tells them: "We've got you, little boo; we're here for a reason, and that reason is you."

When you do this over and over again, **when you take a stand against the things that threaten your audience, a powerful thing happens. You build trust—the real kind.** You demonstrate your commitment. You transform random actions into a cohesive narrative.

Think of it as your version of the Bat-Signal. (See Figure 9.1.)

Figure 9.1. What's your Bat-Signal?

It's the difference between blending the f*ck in and standing the f*ck out. This is what makes a brand so distinctive.

By the way, did you notice what I just did?

I'll give you a few minutes to reread this chapter's start. What I've shared with you so far in this chapter is . . . a **POV**! Why? I claim I understand why you're afraid of alienating customers. Then I describe the thoughts that might go through your mind. I show you I'm on your side. Then I explain the consequences of not having a clear **POV**, and then give you a way to do the same without sounding like a jackass.

To put together your first **POV**, you can follow the **CHIPS** framework (because I like to imagine you eating chips while drafting those), as shown in Figure 9.2. Anyway, it stands for:

- **Common belief.** What others tend to think or do
- **Happen.** What the consequence is as a result
- **Impact.** What the direct effect is on your **segment**
- **Proof.** Why others should believe you (logic, personal anecdotes, stories, stats . . .)
- **Solution.** What should be done instead

Common Belief
Happen
Impact
Proof
Solution

Figure 9.2. Use the CHIPS framework to structure your POV.

Table 9.1. POV Structure Example

CHIPS Framework Phase	Example
Common belief: What others tend to think or do	Brands mistakenly believe a strong **POV** alienates customers.
Happen: What the consequence is as a result	So they play it safe and blend the f*ck in.
Impact: What the direct effect is on your **segment**	Their audience feels confused and uninspired, unable to connect with a brand that doesn't seem to stand for anything.
Proof: Why others should believe you (logic, personal anecdotes, stories, stats . . .)	Logic is used to make the point, as humans have a deep-seated desire for certainty and control—which a **POV** helps to fill.
Solution: What should be done instead	Brands should take a stand against the things that threaten their audience in order to build trust and turn random actions into a cohesive narrative.

Table 9.1 is the typical structure I advise you to use when starting out. You don't have to follow it religiously; it's just a starting point using basic principles of storytelling.

There are a couple of things to remember about your **POV**.

Those messages are there to *protect* your segment from harm by the monster. No matter where you share them, no matter the format, no matter with whom, those signals must link back one way or the other to the **monster** you've identified. It helps you stay on track and it helps you have a genuine **POV** that connects with your people.

And sharing a POV is *not* the same as sharing your opinion or being controversial just to stir the pot so people notice you. It signals a willingness to risk short-term disagreement to build lasting trust, mainly by:

- **Facing the music.** Taking a stand *might* attract criticism from those who disagree.

- **Investing in your beliefs.** Developing and communicating a strong POV often requires significant resources and effort.

- **Focusing your energy.** By focusing on a specific **segment** of the market, you're acknowledging that you *can't* be everything to everyone.

The Plan: Extract Your POV

Step 1. Find Out What Your Segment Hates With Clichés

This method involves identifying what your segment *hates* the most about your category or industry in order to build a narrative that slaps. As in, what annoys your people sooooo much they can't help but talk about it with their neighbor Bernard when he's taking the bins out, even though he has no fucking clue what they're talking about?

I love using this approach because it feels natural and taps into our neg-ativity bias—that human tendency to fixate on the negative. (Just turn on the news for five minutes if you need proof.)

Example:

Let's go back to Jon Goodman, the CEO of the PTDC (Personal Trainer Development Center). We use the cliché method to find content ideas he could share over and over again to become more visible—and trusted.

First, Jon asked his followers on his Facebook page what they hated the most about the fitness industry—without holding back (very important). (See Figure 9.3.)

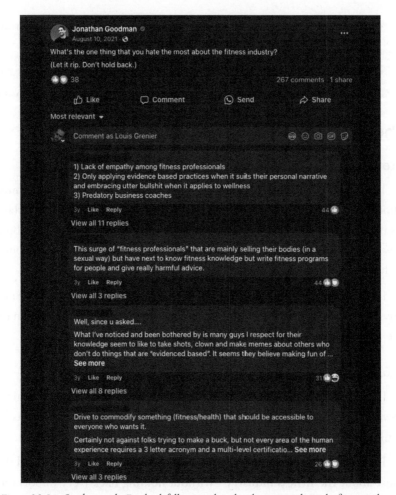

Figure 9.3. Jon Goodman asks Facebook followers what they hate most about the fitness industry.

We analyzed over 250 responses about fitness clichés and discovered five major themes. One of these themes was a *strong* dislike for narcissistic, ego-driven fake gurus who sell sex and fear, flaunting their bodies online and appearing to "win" compared with experienced coaches.

Then we identified the clichés that the PTDC believed to be true, since not everyone may share the same opinion.

And then, since I believe people can't discover their voice and develop their POV in the shadows, I just asked Jon to talk publicly about some of

those clichés. I wanted to see how it felt. He had a large social media following and an active email list, so it didn't take him long.

We used what we learned to formalize a series of POVs that the company could use as the foundation for its entire marketing strategy. For example, let's turn this cliché into a proper **POV**: "The stereotypical perception of health/fitness: people who show off their bodies online 'winning' when compared with an experienced coach. This dilutes the image of a personal trainer or coach." See Table 9.2.

Table 9.2. PTDC POV from Cliché

Phases	Example
Common belief: What others tend to think or do	Most trainers think that, to be taken seriously, they have to flaunt their physique online.
Happen: What the consequence is as a result	Most trainers think that, to be taken seriously, they have to flaunt their physique online.
Impact: What the direct effect is on your **segment**	This makes it hard for them to be seen as a serious professional, which could be holding them back from growing their business.
Proof: Why others should believe you (logic, personal anecdotes, stories, stats . . .)	I've been helping trainers scale their businesses since 2012, and I've noticed something interesting. The ones who truly succeed—the genuinely skilled trainers—prioritize ethics and look exactly like their Instagram pictures.
Solution: What should be done instead	Forget the flash and focus on the fundamentals. It's the boring stuff that matters. The trainers with the most impressive physiques treat fitness as a lifelong journey, not a 30-day challenge.

Jon used the series of POVs we developed to become the face of the brand again, primarily by posting multiple times a day on his personal Instagram where he reached 200,000+ followers.

TAKE ACTION

This exercise helps you tap into what people hate to create a powerful POV. Here's what to do:

1. **Gather the dirt.** Ask the folks in your **segment** what they hate most about your industry or **category**. Encourage raw, unfiltered responses.

2. **Spot the patterns.** Analyze the responses and identify the most common complaints—the big, juicy clichés that make people rant.

3. **Talk about those clichés in the open.**

4. **Transform the clichés** into a set of clear, concise **POV** statements.

My top three clichés are:

1. _____

2. _____

3. _____

Step 2. Unearth Your Own Frustrations

This method flips the script. Instead of digging into what your audience hates, you're going to unearth your own frustrations and opinions to turn them into your POV. This might sound easy peasy lemon squeezy, but it's actually quite challenging. Why? Because we're blind to our own brilliance. We assume that everyone and their dog share our worldview. But here's the kicker: *not everyone does.* Here are three ways to unearth those hidden gems.

1. **Revisit past conversations.**

   Think back to heated debates you've had about your industry or audience:

   - Where did people disagree with you the most?
   - Which of your social media posts, articles, or interviews sparked the most passionate responses?
   - What controversial opinions have you kept bottled up?

2. **Journal through it.**

   All you need is a pen and piece of paper. Start writing whatever comes to mind without any filter or fear of making grammatical mistakes. When I'm feeling very sassy, I tend to write insults until I have none left. After a few minutes, my thoughts start to get clearer. By the time I get to the next page, I feel like I'm in the zone.

   If you're new to this, try to *stay in the moment* to avoid rambling. It may sound a bit weird, I know, so here's what I mean: write down how you feel right now, capture the thoughts that come to mind right in this moment, and stay present.

3. **Get interviewed.**

   Getting interviewed is a smart way to spread your message because you're letting someone else do the heavy lifting. I've seen this firsthand in my coaching sessions. One sales coach I worked with was struggling to define her **POV**. I started asking her simple questions like, "Why are you doing this?" and "What frustrates you most about the sales industry?" She went on a rant—unfiltered and passionate. After a few minutes, she realized how helpful it was to articulate her thoughts out loud.

   Jon Goodman used a similar approach to refine his message. Instead of staying behind the scenes developing courses, he got out there and shared his message. One of his strategies was to appear on established podcasts with over 50 episodes, ensuring he spoke to committed hosts. That gave him the chance to practice, practice,

practice. To sense what was landing and what wasn't. And to adjust his **POV** in real time.

TAKE ACTION

It's time to stop taking your opinions for granted and turn them into a series of reliable signals. Here's what to do:

1. **Reflect on past convos.** Review past debates—online or offline. Where did people disagree with you most? What sparked the most passionate responses?

2. **Do journaling.** Write down every unfiltered, controversial thought you have about your industry or audience. Don't hold back.

3. **Conduct interviews.** Have someone interview you about your work or your clients. If you're being interviewed, ask the person to probe into your frustrations and unpopular opinions.

My strongest opinions are:

1. _____

2. _____

3. _____

Step 3. Find 1,000 Ways to Say the Same Thing

Your **POV** can't just sit in a pretty little slide deck that only you and Geoffrey the intern have access to. Marketing is about making a persuasive argument[43]—not just giving free information—which means your content should support your **POV**.

---

43   Louis Grenier and Billy Broas. 2024. "Funnels Don't Build Businesses: Here's What Does." *Everyone Hates Marketers.* https://podcast.everyonehate smarketers.com/episodes / funnels-dont-build-businesses-heres-what-does.

To make persuasive arguments that generate results *without* ever running out of ideas, you have to find 1,000 ways to share the same perspective. How do you do this? Simply by slicing and dicing your arguments into smaller pieces.

The key is to break down a POV into different components, like slicing an avocado into small cubes. Then, sprinkle it naturally into whatever messages you share, like mixing the small avocado cubes into a salad. For example, you could slice and dice a **POV** in multiple formats, as shown in Figure 9.4.

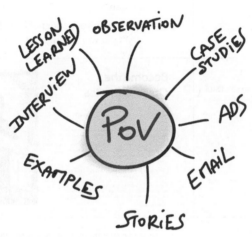

Figure 9.4. Multiple formats can be derived from a single POV.

For example, Coach Goodman believes authenticity, not flashy physiques, builds trust and success for fitness trainers. Table 9.3 shows how he incorporates this belief across various content formats.

Table 9.3. Slicing and Dicing POVs Across Formats

	POV: Authenticity, not flashy physiques, builds trust and success for fitness trainers.
Instagram post about winning your community before trying to win the internet	**Jonathan Goodman** @itscoachgoodman IG is a colossal waste of time for most trainers. You don't need to be an influencer. $108,000/yr = 30 clients * $300/month Try to win your community before trying to win the internet.
Homepage section building a business versus becoming an online entertainer	**Become the Obvious Choice** Trying to win the internet is a gloriously inefficient way to build a business. Forget becoming an influencer. Just because you can sell to the world, it doesn't mean that you have to--and it's definitely not where you start. Building a business and becoming an online entertainer are different games people play--neither's better or worse but problems arise when you conflate the two--playing by the rules of one and desiring the rewards of the other. It's not about being the best choice for everyone. It's about being the obvious choice for the right people. Whether you're new or you've been on this journey for years, I want to show you all the ways you can succeed on your own terms: without compromising personal relationships, wellbeing, and your quality of life. Here's what I mean:
Email newsletter about being rich in likes versus being poor in dollars	**How to Avoid Being Rich with Likes but Poor with Dollars** Click here if you prefer to read it on the website (or send to a friend) Jessica was a struggling online coach with only 6 paying clients. *"My issues are marketing and sales. I need a social media manager, more professional photos of myself, and more time."* She said. She had 20,600 followers on Instagram when I got her message. That's enough people to fill Madison Square Garden. If we assume that her 6 clients came directly from social media, her conversion rate is 0.029%, or 1 client for every 3,433 followers. **Adding free followers isn't Jessica's issue; getting paying clients is.** Despite prevailing wisdom, they aren't the same thing. Jessica's rich with likes but poor with dollars.

The three examples featured in Table 9.3 all stem from the same **POV**. Jon may not explicitly mention it every time, but it's *always* there.

The key lesson here is that your POV must always be present. However, it shouldn't be the *main* ingredient (like avocado cubes in a salad). It's there to support whatever you're putting out into the world.

Here's what I like to do when working with new clients who don't know where to begin with this **POV** thingy. First, we make a list of the assets that their **segment** sees the most. Things like the website homepage, product packaging, transactional emails (like purchase confirmation), and so on. Then we look into inserting their **POV** within each of those assets. We don't obsess over making the **POV** the main ingredient. Instead, we just try to find ways to weave it in. Finally, we reflect on how it feels to add it.

Whatever you pick should free you from thinking that repeating yourself is a bad thing.

TAKE ACTION

Repeating your message is critical, but no one wants to hear the same thing over and over. This exercise helps you share your **POV** in fresh ways across your content.

Here's what to do:

1. **Identify key assets.** List the content your audience sees most (website, emails, social media, etc.).

2. **Choose your POV.** Select one **POV** you want to weave into your content.

3. **Get slicing and dicing.** Think of three to five different ways to express your chosen **POV**. Think stories, examples, questions, or even metaphors.

4. **Start the infusion.** Add your sliced and diced **POV** variations into your chosen assets. How does it feel? Does it sound natural and engaging?

The Doubts: "What if I'm Not a Contrarian Like You?"

"Won't people stop following me if I repeat myself too much?"

No, people won't stop following you because you repeated something. Quite the opposite. Yes, they might know that thing already, but repeating it *your way* helps them learn it. Yes, they might have known that thing before but probably forgot about it. Yes, every day, fresh faces show up in your world, knowing zilch, and they need to hear from you. And yes, the people you look up to repeat themselves constantly.

Science backs this up: the more we *see* something, the more we tend to *like* it. This cognitive bias, known as the mere exposure effect, has even been proven with meaningless symbols. In one experiment,[44] people were shown characters that looked like Chinese symbols and asked to guess their meaning. Those who saw the same symbols repeatedly were more likely to associate them with positive meanings. This suggests that even subconscious familiarity can influence our preferences.

In other words, one message shared many times is far more powerful than many messages shared once.

"I'm an introvert so I don't want to have a POV."

I believe being an introvert is a superpower, not a weakness. It means you have the ability to observe, reflect, and come up with unique insights the extroverts might miss. You don't have to be loud to have a strong **POV**. Use your unique insights to craft a perspective that resonates with the folks in your **segment**. Show them you understand their **struggles** and you're in their corner. Embrace your introversion and communicate in a way that feels authentic to you.

---

44 American Psychological Association. "Attitudinal Effects of Mere Exposure." https://psycnet. apa.or g/record/1968-12019-001.

"I'm not aggressive or contrarian like you."

Look, this book is not about me. It's not about giving you a recipe that will turn you into a French intellectual terrorist. No, it's deeper than that. It's a framework for you to explore the limits. *Your* limits. It's a framework for positioning your business, finding your people, and standing the f*ck out in crowded markets. The possibilities are endless.

"I don't want to take a stand. I believe everything is more nuanced."

Having a **POV** isn't about ignoring nuance—the opposite, in fact. It's about *acknowledging* nuance. It's about taking a clear stance on what matters most to your **segment**, giving those in your **segment** comfort, and sending long-term signals to show you're in their corner. Try to use your nuanced thinking to craft a **POV** that acknowledges complexity while providing clear guidance. Your **segment** will appreciate your authenticity.

"I'm going to piss people off, not sell, and then go bankrupt."

I can count on one hand the number of times I've received backlash for sharing my **POV** over the last decade (and by "backlash," I mean a couple of emails from folks who just didn't agree—that's it).

If you speak to your **segment** with a relatable **POV** without insulting others, you have nothing to worry about. The long-term benefits—getting noticed, being believed, building trust, and having fun—far outweigh the possible short-term challenges.

The Recap: Are You a Hermit Crab?

Remember that hermit crab, too scared to leave its shell? That's your brand without a **POV**. In this chapter, we've learned to send clear signals that tell your people you're on their side, ready to protect them from the **monsters** lurking in your **category**.

Let's recap the key takeaways:

- **Ditch the random opinions and build a POV.** A **POV** is a collection of consistent messages woven into everything you do, signaling to the people in your segment that you're there to protect them.

- **Use the CHIPS framework to structure your POV.** Common belief, Happen (consequence), Impact, Proof, Solution.

- **There are three ways to extract your POV.** Uncover what your **segment** hates, unearth your own frustrations, and find 1,000 ways to say the same thing.

- **Don't be afraid to repeat yourself.** Sharing one message many times is more powerful than sharing many messages once.

- **Having a POV is not about being a French contrarian.** It's about taking a stand on what matters most to your **segment**, even if it makes some people uncomfortable.

10

The Spices

Some people think Seth Godin is a marketer for non-marketers—that he lacks the hands-on, practical experience to be credible nowadays. They complain you have to read between the lines or figure things out yourself.

I'd say they're missing the point.

Seth intentionally avoids giving you a detailed road map. Instead, he challenges you to *think* on your own because that's how real learning happens. I experienced this firsthand with one of Seth's lessons, which stuck with me so profoundly that it inspired this entire chapter.

In his book *Purple Cow,* Seth says:

> "Companies that are built around mass marketing develop their products accordingly. These companies round the edges, smooth out the differentiating features, and try to make products that are bland enough to work for the masses. **These companies make spicy food less spicy**, and they make insanely great service a little less great (and a little cheaper). They push everything—from the price to the performance—to the center of the market."

(I added the boldface.)

The Problem: Talk Is Cheap . . .

Let's continue with the spicy food analogy. You can't run a Pakistani restaurant, tell everyone that your Sindhi biryani is the spiciest around—and then *not* add the red chili powder because you're afraid your patrons won't like it.

You want the folks in your segment to feel like you genuinely get them, you're in their corner, and you prove it with your actions. Talk is cheap, right? *Anyone* can say *anything*. But when you operate as if marketing is all about communication and nothing else, you enter a dangerous cycle:

- You're forced to make stupid promises to your audience.

- You have to interrupt as many people as possible, hoping something sticks.

- Results are mediocre (or worse).

- There's no budget left to actually do better.

- The gap between what you say and what you do keeps getting wider.

- Pressure intensifies.

Rinse, repeat.

Your **distinctive brand** is *everything* you do (and don't do). Brands that stand the f*ck out tend to have something in common: there's virtually no gap between what they say, how they're perceived, and what they actually do—as shown in Figure 10.1.

Figure 10.1. A distinctive brand closely matches its words with its actions.

For example, imagine if Daft Punk, the French electronic duo, came out of retirement to chase fame, removing their $65,000 helmets in the process? Or if Seth Godin was announcing on his blog that he struck a deal with a major crypto trading website? Impossible, right?

Because there seems to be little to no difference between what they say, how they're perceived, and what they actually do. **The real challenge with standing the f*ck out is to align what you *say* with what you *do*. Make it so your people know you're there for them.**

The Solution: . . . But Action Is Spicy!

Studies show that once we believe in a part of our identity (*I'm a cook who uses a lot of spices*), we're more likely to act in sync with it (as with pushing past your fear to make your Sindhi biryani the spiciest in town; some can't handle the heat as you become "too spicy," but for others, it's like, "Finally! A Sindhi biryani that is spicy af!").[45]

---

45 Research shows that framing voting as part of one's identity ("being a voter") rather than just an action ("voting") can increase voter registration interest and actual turnout. This demonstrates how subtle changes in language can influence behavior by appealing to people's self-image. Christopher J. Bryan et al., "Motivating Voter Turnout by Invoking the Self," *Proceedings of the National Academy of Sciences* 108, no. 31 (2011): 12653–12656

Introducing spices: the tangible actions you take that bring your POVs to life in a way your specific segment will notice. The big players in your market try to please everyone, so they're unlikely to turn up the heat. That's another advantage you have as an underdog.

> While your **POV** is there to send trusting signals, **spices** are what allow you to back them up.

Find your **spice** using the following structure: *We are too (adverb) + (adjective).*

For example, my Sindhi biryani is *too dangerously spicy* because very few can handle the heat. And this book is *too gloriously profane* for folks with delicate sensibilities.

A good **spice** follows the **SPICE**[46] framework, as visualized in Figure 10.2.

- **Stands the test of time.** Resist changing it every six months. Think of it as the bedrock of your brand—a solid foundation that everyone internally can rally behind. Don't mess with it, please.

- **Pushes you to the very edge of the map** (where no one else is). Imagine a map of possibilities. Go far beyond the well-trodden paths, to the very edge where you—and only you—have ever been. It acts as a constant reminder to stand the f*ck out.

- **Is unclaimable by others.** It should be distinct and not something that big brands or **alternatives** can easily replicate or claim as their own. I mean, yes, they could easily *talk* about it, but can they actually behave that way? The bigger they are, the more difficult it's going to be for them.

- **Characterizes specific behaviors.** It should clearly articulate what you're going to do and how you're going to do it. Because, remember: talk is cheap.

---

46 Thank you Ant Bailey-Grice for helping me come up with this acronym.

- **Easy to understand and apply.** It's straightforward enough for you, or your team, or your client to grasp quickly and use as a guiding principle for *daily* actions.

Figure 10.2. Structure your spices using the SPICE framework.

Example:

I recently worked with a SaaS founder selling an all-in-one platform for coaches. He kept telling me that his customer support was exceptional and that customers raved about it. Honestly, it just didn't sound true to me; every tech company out there claims the same thing. So I asked him to explain *exactly* what he meant.

He told me that the folks who answer customers' emails are not there to send canned responses but to coach them so they feel understood and less alone since entrepreneurship is very lonely for them (they don't have a strong support network). The potential **spices** we came up with are in Table 10.1.

Table 10.1. Evaluating Potential Spices for the All-in-One Coaching Platform

Potential Alternatives	Comments
Too customer-centric	**Incorrect**. Every company out there claims the exact same thing. It's bland as fuck.

Potential Alternatives	Comments
Too synergistically supportive	**Incorrect**. It's too buzzwordy. Need I say more?
Too intimately caring	**Correct**. It correctly describes how deep they go to help their customers feel less lonely and more successful.

Example:

If we go back to the Danbury Trashers story, we can infer that they were *too unapologetically aggressive.* This highlights the team's on-ice behavior, record-setting penalties, and willingness to embrace a rough-and-tough style of hockey to entertain their fans. Other hockey teams in their division could not, in good faith, claim the same thing.

The Plan: Two Steps to Uncover Spices

Step 1. Channel Your Alter Ego

My favorite method to extract spices is to identify an *alter ego* that possesses the qualities you want to embody. This whole exercise might feel weird, so here's a way to overcome this mental barrier. In *The Alter Ego Effect*, Todd Herman—a coach for elite athletes—advises channeling an alter ego that possesses the qualities you feel you're missing.

Think of it like Superman—mild-mannered Clark Kent steps into a phone booth and emerges as the hero. You're doing that, but mentally. I also love to think of the quiet and shy Farrokh Bulsara who routinely transformed into one of the greatest performers of all time when stepping into the role of Freddie Mercury. I mean, have you seen his performance at Live Aid in 1985?[47] I've just rewatched it while writing this, and wow . . . the goosebumps! Unreal!

Here's how to develop an *alter ego* to uncover **spices.**

---

47 "Queen—Bohemian Rhapsody (Live Aid)." 1985. YouTube. https://www.youtube.com/watch?v=vbvyNnw8Qjg.

First, think about the qualities you want to embody that you may struggle with. Think about what may hold you back from standing the f*ck out. For example, you may struggle to speak in public and want to be seen as a more confident public speaker. Or your hockey team is not aggressive enough and you want your players to become more hostile when they're on the ice.

Then, visualize a character who embodies those qualities. It could be a superhero version of yourself (like Clark Kent and Superman), it could be a fictional character, or it could be a real person. Take inspiration from artists, mavericks, brands, politicians, creators, athletes, historical figures, or cartoon characters outside of your field that *you* admire and would like to emulate. Go deep. Visualize how they carry themselves, how they dress, how they speak, what superpowers they may have.

Finally, choose a name for your character and create its backstory. This is how you make it real and trick your brain into thinking this *alter ego* exists. I mean, when Farrokh Bulsara was on stage, I'm 100 percent sure he believed *in his bones* he was the flamboyant Freddie Mercury.

Example:

My friend Shanty went from baking in her kitchen to building and selling a multimillion-euro food brand in just 10 years (see Figure 10.3). She's among the most creative and courageous entrepreneurs I've ever met. Her secret? She has an alter ego, the *Bisqueen* (biscuit + queen).

Figure 10.3. Shanty Baehrel in her first workshop back in 2017.

When Covid hit, Shanty Biscuits had to shut down production at its factory in France. The company couldn't sell anything, so Shanty switched focus to keeping the *brand* alive. While other brands were turning up the anxiety factor to 11 on social media—lockdowns, social distancing, and masks—she channeled the *Bisqueen* and chose another path.

What if she never, ever, ever talked about Covid on Instagram, where most of the audience was? What if the *Bisqueen* doubled down on bringing joy, laughter, and good vibes?

While other brands reminded their followers that social distance was 2 meters minimum, she launched the Shanty Challenge, asking people to eat biscuits off their foreheads without using their hands. She also created song parodies with her sister and hosted fashion shows with bubble wrap.

Free from the pressure of selling, comfy in her home studio and lifted up by her online community, the *Bisqueen's* creativity took off. With time and space to play, her imagination went wild, and her audience loved it.

She's the motherfucking *Bisqueen*. A creative contrarian who does things others wouldn't even dare to put on Post-it notes in a brainstorming meeting. If I had to come up with a **spice** for her, it would be *too creatively defiant*.

TAKE ACTION

Channel your inner rockstar to uncover hidden qualities. Here's what to do:

1. **Identify what holds you back.** What qualities do you want to possess to stand the f*ck out?

2. **Create your alter ego.** Imagine a character—real or fictional—who embodies those qualities. Get vivid and picture that character's look, attitude, even superpowers.

3. **Give your alter ego a name and a backstory.** Make this alter ego feel real. What's your alter ego's name? What's your alter ego's story?

4. **Infer spices.** Channel your alter ego. What **spices** manifest? How would your alter ego act in this situation?

Step 2. Turn Spices into Real Behavior

To stand the f*ck out, your **spices** must not just sit on pretty slides in a brand book nobody reads. Those **spices** should be the cornerstone of your standing the f*ck out process so every team member sees them every day and understands that those **spices** are part of who *they* are.

To make **spices** actionable for everyone, I like to use this structure:

- **Action:** What we'll do because of this **spice**

- **Inaction:** What we won't do because of this **spice**

- **Example:** A real-life example of the action in practice

In Table 10.2, I share examples of turning **spices** into real behavior.

Table 10.2. Examples of Making Spices Actionable

Spice	Action	Inaction	Example
Danbury Trashers: We are too unapologetically aggressive.	Prank visiting teams as often as possible. Recruit players who are amazing fighters. Intimidate everyone.	Won't play to win Won't focus on becoming a more skilled player (focus on being a better fighter)	Turning off the hot water in the other team's locker room
Shanty the Bisqueen: I am too creatively defiant.	Focus on having fun, not trying to sell something.	Won't talk about Covid, masks, lockdowns	Shanty Challenge: Take a biscuit, put it on your forehead, eat without hands.
This book: It's too gloriously profane.	Use swear words to make a point, and write like I speak.	Won't use buzzwords to sound smart	This entire book, I guess?

TAKE ACTION

Your brand's **spices** shouldn't just sit on a shelf.

Here's what to do:

1. **List your spices.** Write down the key characteristics or values that define your brand.

2. **For each spice, define:**
   - Action. What you'll do because of this spice
   - Inaction. What you won't do because of this spice
   - Example. A real-life example of the action in practice

3. **Create a table.** Organize your spices, actions, inactions, and examples into a table format for easy reference.

4. **Share with your team.** Distribute this table to all and discuss how to incorporate these behaviors into the day-to-day.

My **spices** and their actionable behaviors:

Spice 1: too _____

Action: _____

Inaction: _____

Example: _____

(Repeat for additional **spices**.)

The Doubts: "I'm Sorry but This All Feels Too Weird . . ."

"I want everyone to agree with me."

By "everyone," I mean your colleagues, boss, friends, lunch lady . . . You may struggle to stand the f*ck out because you are afraid of being judged. This fear of judgment runs incredibly deep because we're a social species that needs to belong. Nowadays I'm trying to fight it; I accept it for what it is and channel it in a positive way. If some people find my ideas ridiculous/stupid/too much/too aggressive/[insert anything else people come up with], I take it as a good sign.

"My industry is super boring, so I can't do any of that."

Lucky you! I *wish* I were in a *boring* industry; it means there are more opportunities to stand out because companies tend to play safe. When I hear "boring," it usually means a sector that's been around for a while, with proven demand and established competition. This means you can lean on what's already there and figure out ways to make it work for yourself.

"We already have a set of brand values; do I really need to work on those, too?"

I'm not a big fan of values because they tend to be super vague, which means that they are unactionable for folks involved.

I find **spices** to be more potent because they (1) describe a specific behavior as part of an identity and (2) challenge you to make your spicy food *more* spicy, to go to the edge of the map where no one else is.

"I feel weird developing an alter ego. Can I skip this step?"

You're welcome to follow the steps you want; I ain't your boss . . . But here's something to consider. If you feel uneasy working on it, if you're wary about others' reactions, it might mean that you're finally doing things you are not used to, which, in turn, means you're on the path to stand the f*ck out. Because if it was easy, everyone would do it, amirite?

The Recap: Serve the Spiciest Sindhi Biryani

Talk is cheap. Your actions must match your words. This chapter is about adding **spices**: tangible actions that prove you're different. Big players play it safe—your advantage is to crank up the heat.

Let's recap the key takeaways from this chapter:

- **Close the gap.** Align what you say, how you're perceived, and what you actually do.

- **Spice it up.** Define your brand's unique flavor with the **SPICE** formula:

  ○ Stands the test of time
  ○ Pushes you to the edge
  ○ Is unclaimable by others
  ○ Characterizes specific behaviors
  ○ Easy to understand and apply

- **Unleash your alter ego.** Identify the qualities you want to embody, and create a character who embodies them. What would your character—*alter ego*—do?

- **Turn spices into action.** Define what you will and won't do because of your **spice**. Give real-life examples.

- **Embrace the weird.** If it feels uncomfortable, you're probably on the right track.

11

The Assets

OK—we have a **monster** to rally people around, a **POV** to send trusted signals to the people in our **segment**, and **spices** to back them up with real behavior. Now let's talk about branding.

Rewind to the days of my tragically flawed marketing agency. I was thinking about building a software solution called "Slices," a tool for e-commerce businesses to use to dissect data and personalize customer communication.

I thought the name was clever since it referred to *slicing* and dicing data. When I pivoted to offering services, "Slices" and its scalpel logo (as shown in Figure 11.1) made perfect sense to me.

Figure 11.1. Slices logo.

But it also *tasted* about as exciting as a glass of tap water. **Psychophysicist Mark Changizi[48] explains that water tastes like "nothing" because our brains are hardwired to perceive it that way—and not because it lacks flavor.** Basically, any hint of a different taste could signal danger, so our brains default to neutral to keep us safe. Back in the day, this was a matter of survival.

The same principle applies to your branding. If it looks, feels, and tastes like everything else—like lukewarm water—it's *invisible*. People's brains won't even register it.

The Problem: We Try Too Hard to Be Meaningful

And that's what happens when branding tries too hard to be meaningful. Like my old agency and its scalpel. Or copywriters using fountain pens as their logo. Or those nonfiction books using "f*ck" in their title (oops).

Research about how our brains work shows that we *don't* buy things based on the meaning of a brand. You don't hire FedEx to deliver a package because its logo has a hidden arrow. You don't buy chocolate bars from Toblerone because the yellow mountain is actually a bear.[49] And you didn't choose to read this book because there's a rooster on the cover (his name is Roger, by the way).

Worse than that, choosing a branding asset based on a *preexisting* meaning could harm you because it may:

- **Clog your customer's brain.** Instead of your brand popping into your customer's head, you might also compete with other memories associated with an **asset** that have *nothing* to do with your **category**. Which might make it harder for customers to remember and choose you.

---

48 As mentioned by Rory Sutherland in *Alchemy: The Surprising Power of Ideas That Don't Make Sense*. Ebury Publishing, 2019.

49 The bear is the animal that represents the canton of Bern, where Toblerone comes from.

- **Make you a copycat.** If you're chasing the same meanings as an **alternative**, you risk arriving at the same exact point[50] and looking like a cheap imitation.

- **Go stale.** Today's hot topic is tomorrow's old news. Building your brand on a trend is like building a house on sand—it's unlikely to last.

In other words: meaning, in and of itself, doesn't mean shit.

The Solution: Be Meaning-Free

You see, we pick a certain category or brand because something within us or our environment—where we are, who we're with, what we see—triggers something. *Not* because of some deeper meaning.

> Assets are the distinctive bits and bobs that make your brand uniquely yours—could be a color, shape, sound, word, or even a mascot. The goal? Create meaning-free brand assets that tickle different parts of the brain.[51] Why? Because it helps build stronger memory structures *without* competing with all the other crap floating around in people's heads.

A bit more neuroscience to back this up:

- **Faces.** We're hardwired to notice them thanks to the fusiform gyrus in our brains.

- **Colors.** Colors are processed in the occipital lobe, with different neurons responding to various light wavelengths.

- **Phrases.** Phrases are handled by Broca's area (for speaking) and Wernicke's area (for understanding).

---

50 Unique brand assets are more memorable. Designs similar to those of competitors can blur recall, making your brand less distinct in people's minds.

51 I first learned about this idea in Jenni Romaniuk's book, *Building Distinctive Brand Assets.* Oxford University Press, 2018.

Figure 11.2 is my attempt to show you where those areas are in the brain.

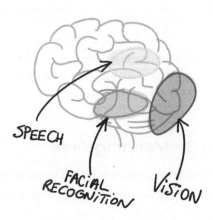

Figure 11.2. Approximate areas of the brain dedicated to recognizing faces, colors, and phrases.

In other words, your branding assets should work together to have the highest chance of being noticed and building stronger memory structures.

Before going further, let me clear up something. I'm not saying go completely bonkers with random branding. A trash can logo for a tech-focused accounting firm? Probably not. But find that sweet spot—recognizable *yet* distinctive. Challenge *some* **category** conventions, but not *all*. You don't want to confuse people to the point where they're scratching their heads, wondering what the hell you are.

Take the Danbury Trashers. Their logo? A mean-looking, animated steel trash can (as shown in Figure 11.3).

Figure 11.3. The Danbury Trashers logo.[52]

What are the chances that any other hockey teams, let alone sports teams, use the same? Zero to none. But the Trashers kept the hockey stick, grounding it in their **category**. It's unexpected and distinctive, without leaving people clueless about the sport they play.

Of course, nothing is entirely meaning-free, but explore branding elements that don't scream what you do. It's about being distinctive, not obvious. With that in mind, Jenni Romaniuk in *How Brands Grow (Part 2)* advises to design a diverse palette of distinctive **assets** with the following elements:

- A color (or a color combination)
- A logo or shape
- Something with a face (a character or spokesperson)
- A sound
- A short phrase

Combining each of those elements creates a solid starting point for being distinctive—yet highly recognizable.

---

52   Thank you A.J. Galante for allowing me to use the logo in the book.

Example:

I realized last year that my own brand needed a refresh. I wasn't practicing the very principles I preached.

So, I challenged myself to go to the edge of the map and find the most **distinctive brand assets** possible in a super-crowded **category**. I wanted to be very deliberate and intentional by doubling down on elements I knew were working while developing others that had huge potential. I ended up developing the branding kit in Table 11.1.

Table 11.1. My Distinctive Branding

Asset Types	Stand The F*ck Out Assets
A color (or a color combination)	Black, orange, purple A bit flashy for my **category**, but it's not unique.
A logo or shape	Sticker-style graphics, mimicking the appearance and qualities of physical stickers
Something with a face (a character or spokesperson)	Roger the Rooster, my French rooster with a questionable fashion sense It's not totally meaning-free since a French rooster connects with my nationality. But it's not directly related to what I do for work, which makes it very unlikely that anyone else in my category will use it.
A sound	My French accent. I used to hate it; I even tried to suppress it. But then I realized it was something that others noticed. So I doubled down on it.
A short phrase	Stand The F*ck Out. *Duh.*

Say *bonjour* to Roger—Figure 11.4.

Figure 11.4. Roger the Rooster and his distinctive purple béret

Example:

Picture this: launching a business with just $250, in the wake of Hurricane Katrina, in an industry you're clueless about. Now imagine turning that gamble into a multimillion-dollar brand. This is the story of Demo Diva, where Simone Bruni (pictured in Figure 11.5) didn't just enter the demolition industry—she smashed through it like a wrecking ball (cue Miley Cyrus).

Figure 11.5. Simone Bruni, aka Demo Diva.

"For the first few years, I operated on a shoestring budget," Simone admits.[53] "I didn't even think about branding. 'Demo Diva' felt kitschy; I saw it as a temporary gig until I could get back on my feet." Her early branding efforts? Pink T-shirts. "If you worked for me, you wore the shirt," Simone told me.

And then one day at the drive-thru, a cashier recognized her as *the* Demo Diva. That's when the shift happened. Simone invested in her first pink excavator. She went all in. See Demo Diva's distinctive branding in all its glory in Table 11.2.

Table 11.2. Demo Diva's Distinctive Branding Assets

Asset Types	Demo Diva's Assets
A color (or a color combination)	Pink Virtually everyone else in the demolition sector uses black and yellow.
A logo or shape	n/a
Something with a face (a character or spokesperson)	Simone Bruni herself The demolition industry's branding conventions are generally "faceless."
A sound	n/a
A short phrase	*Takin' It Down to the Dirt.* This is a fun catchphrase, which again stands out against competitors.

53 Louis Grenier and Simone Bruni. 2023. "Smashing Norms: How to Craft Stand-The-F*ck-Out Brands in Old-School Industries." *Everyone Hates Marketers.* https://podcast. everyonehatesmarketers.com/episodes/smashing-norms-how-to-craft-stand-the-f-ck-out-brands-in-old-school-industries.

The Plan: Develop Meaning-Free Assets

Step 1. Pay Attention to What Others Notice

This method is about identifying and exaggerating your most distinctive traits to identify branding elements that stand the f*ck out. Think of it like a caricature artist who would stare into your soul to amplify what makes you, or your brand, or your client, *unique*.

Everyone with a brain and an internet connection can compete against you and add more noise. As underdogs, we must do the emotional labor on behalf of the people we seek to serve so they get exposed only to what really matters. In other words, we must caricature ourselves to be noticed and understood quickly by our people.

To do this, *don't* just pick random stuff to magnify. Instead, pay attention to what others notice about you, your brand, your product, and so on. It could be anything from a story you told at a conference, a little panda bear you've been using in one of your presentations, or an accent your customers comment on . . . don't take those for granted. You're used to them, of course. But for others, they're new and distinctive.

I know it's a tough exercise because I see it trip people up all the time. Whenever I send a questionnaire to onboard a new client, this question is where most people struggle: "What is one small detail about you or your brand that people often notice?" They either blank or reply with something very mundane, such as, "We are hands-on as owners."

With that in mind, let me give you three pointers.

Don't try to come up with rational *arguments* that you'd use on a sales call—like how hands-on you are as owners. Instead, aim to find little things that don't make a ton of sense and that people do notice.

Which brings me to my second point: Ask people around you what *they* notice. You're unlikely to be a good judge since you're in the midst of it. You can't see the forest for the trees.

What small things about your area of focus tend to catch people's attention? A team member who doubles as an Elvis wedding act?[54] A Canadian copywriter who turned his love for red-and-black plaid shirts into a distinctive look?[55]

And finally, third, let your brand breathe!! Don't take it so fucking seriously. Try new things. Let loose.

> Shortly after launching my podcast *Everyone Hates Marketers*, I started to say, "Bonjour bonjour" at the start of every interview. I just did it because I felt like it. That's it; there was no grand plan behind it. A few weeks after, I noticed that folks were using it at the start of their emails to me. Or on calls. It was a little accident that others paid attention to, so I doubled down on it.

54 Louis Grenier and Dan Kelsall. 2020. "How to Offend People and Create Great F*cking Content." *Everyone Hates Marketers.* https://podcast.everyonehates marketers.com/ episodes/ how-to-offend- people-and-create-great-f-cking-content.

55 Joel Klettke used consistent visual elements (square glasses, plaid shirt, bald) and used them all over LinkedIn. https://twitter.com/JoelKlettke/status/1735697522960838755.

TAKE ACTION

Identify distinctive traits that others notice about you or your brand.

Here's what to do:

1. **Reflect on feedback.** Think about comments or observations others have made about you, your brand, or your products.

2. **Ask for input.** Reach out to colleagues, clients, or friends and ask what they find unique or memorable about you or your brand.

3. **List distinctive traits.** Write down the quirky details that people have noticed. These could be:

   - A catchphrase you use
   - A visual element in your presentations
   - A personal habit or style choice

My distinctive traits are:

- _____
- _____
- _____
- _____

Step 2. Explore the Negative Space

This method helps you uncover hidden gems by pinpointing the branding elements your competitors are overlooking. This untapped territory is the negative space, and it's where you may find opportunities to stand the f*ck out.

First, make a list of the main competitors in your category. If there are thousands, either pick the biggest, most popular ones, or use your knowledge of the sector to create a caricature of it. List what's typically done in terms of:

- Colors

- Logos or shapes
- Characters
- Sounds
- Short phrases

Example:

Let's go back to Simone Bruni and the demolition sector around New Orleans. Her competitors are typically run by alpha males and their brands, and machinery is typically yellow and black. See Table 11.3 for a quick 'n' dirty summary.

Table 11.3. Typical Branding Assets from Demolition Companies

Asset Types	Typical Demolition Company
A color (or a color combination)	Yellow, black
A logo or shape	Excavator
Something with a face (a character or spokesperson)	Wannabe alpha males
A sound	
A short phrase	Strong language like "caveman" or "big boy"

This is where it becomes fun! Take each common **asset** you've found and see how you could go in the opposite direction, as shown in Table 11.4.

Table 11.4. Typical Branding Versus Negative Space from Demolition Companies

Asset Types	Typical Demolition Company	Demo Diva
A color (or a color combination)	Yellow, black	Pink

Asset Types	Typical Demolition Company	Demo Diva
A logo or shape	Excavator	
Something with a face (a character or spokesperson)	Wannabe alpha males	Simone Bruni
A sound		
A short phrase	Strong language like "caveman" or "big boy"	Softer language

It might sound super obvious with the benefit of hindsight since you now know the story of Demo Diva, but I believe this *isn't* an exercise that many of the top dogs have ever used. It doesn't have to be that complicated.

Also, remember my point about finding a balance so you're recognizable but still distinctive? Well, Simone did *not* challenge every single branding convention of the **category**. She uses "Demo" in her name and the same equipment as others in the field, so people understand what she's about. No confusion, just clarity with a unique twist.

This approach also showcases her expertise. Imagine if she used only tiny little excavators because they looked "cuter"—it might raise eyebrows about her capabilities. Instead, Simone demolishes unnecessary stereotypes in the industry, not the practical realities. She's a skilled professional, just with a fresher, bolder approach.

Example:

Allow me to introduce another marketing agency example. When I discovered the Manchester-based ad agency Dark Horse,[56] I fell in love at first sight.

Before I show you how Dark Horse's branding looks, let's think about what you typically expect to see when landing on the website of a typical medium-sized advertising agency. What comes to mind, specifically?

---

56 Find out more about them here: https://darkhorse.co/.

- A row of logos of the agency's best clients?
- Some ultra-specific and ultra-impressive results like "91.74 percent increase in ROAS (return on ad spend)" or "57.90 percent increase in keywords on page 1"?
- Some awards you've never, ever, ever heard of?
- A picture of the team playing air hockey on a night out?
- Some neutral colors like dark blue and white?
- Serious, semi-professional tone of voice?
- All of the above?

Let's map all of that to the asset types in Table 11.5.

Table 11.5. Typical Branding Assets from Local Ad Agencies

Asset Types	Typical Local Ad Agency
A color (or a color combination)	Blue, white
A logo or shape	Logos, lots of them
Something with a face (a character or spokesperson)	Team members smiling at the camera
A sound	
A short phrase	"91.74 percent increase in ROAS"

Yeah, me too.

And now there's Dark Horse with its "detective board" aesthetic, which immediately creates an intense atmosphere (see Figure 11.6). Its website is full of layered information like photos, newspaper clippings, and maps. Interconnected elements linked by strings or markers. Handwritten notes and sketches. A monochromatic color scheme (black and white with a dash of red).

Talk about *not* tasting like water.

Figure 11.6. Dark Horse's "detective board" aesthetic.

OK, now let's compare the typical branding from local ad agencies with Dark Horse in Table 11.6.

Table 11.6. Typical Branding from Local Ad Agencies Versus Dark Horse

Asset Types	Typical Local Ad Agency	Dark Horse
A color (or a color combination)	Blue, white	Monochromatic with a dash of red
A logo or shape	Logos, lots of them	Photos, newspaper clippings, and maps Interconnected elements linked by strings or markers Handwritten notes and sketches
Something with a face (a character or spokesperson)	Team members smiling at the camera, gathered round laptops pretending there was something on the screen and "strategizing"	Ghosts, skulls, dodgy characters from horror movies

Asset Types	Typical Local Ad Agency	Dark Horse
A sound		
A short phrase	"91.74 percent increase in ROAS"	Gritty, visceral copy like, "Forensically good PPC & SEO. We help aspiring e-commerce companies parade the bodies of their competition while swimming in money, through PPC, Paid Social, and SEO."

Gritty, visceral copy like, "Forensically good PPC & SEO. We help aspiring e-commerce companies parade the bodies of their competition while swimming in money, through PPC, Paid Social, and SEO."

Did Dark Horse go too far? What about the balance between being recognizable and being distinctive as an ad agency? This is where I feel the folks at Dark Horse have done an excellent job. Yes, they went all in with the "detective board" style, but still followed **category** conventions. They immediately mention what they do ("Forensically good PPC & SEO"). Their website architecture is exactly what you'd expect from a typical agency, with pages dedicated to their services, such as content marketing or digital PR, the type of ads they run (such as Instagram advertising), or their locations. They also feature their certification logos even though they're buried deep in the footer. And their copy is very much on point, highlighting how they're different from others and how it's a compelling reason for readers to pick them over the competition. They still are part of the game. But they play with some of the rules, you know?

TAKE ACTION

Explore the negative space in your **category's** branding to identify distinctive opportunities.

Here's what to do:

1. **List competitors.** Write down three to five main competitors in your **category**.

2. **Identify typical branding.** For each competitor, note its:
   - Colors
   - Logos or shapes
   - Characters or spokespersons
   - Sounds (if applicable)
   - Short phrases or slogans

3. **Create a summary table.** Compile the common branding elements across competitors.

4. **Explore opposites.** For each common element, brainstorm opposite or contrasting ideas.

My "negative" branding assets are:

- _____
- _____
- _____
- _____

Step 3. List All Potential Assets and Pick One or Two

In this last step, we're going to pick the **assets** that are most likely to stand the f*ck out.

First, list all the potential **assets** you've brainstormed. Don't worry about being perfect yet; just get everything down. Next, choose a few **assets** that connect through a common theme. For the Danbury Trashers, the theme is "trash." For the agency Dark Horse, it's "detective board."

To help you choose between different **assets**, consider these criteria:

- **Uniqueness.** Is this combination of **assets** *unique* within your industry? It's OK if similar elements exist elsewhere, but your specific mix should be distinctive.

- **Nervousness.** Does this kit excite you and your team? Do you feel a little nervous? Are you having heated debates with colleagues or clients about whether this branding should see the light of day? Well, I see that as a good sign. If it's too safe, it might not be distinctive enough.

Remember, choosing your brand **assets** is a balancing act. You want to go very, very far in a couple of dimensions, yet you still want to be recognizable within your **category**.

TAKE ACTION

Select distinctive **assets** that align with a common theme.

Here's what to do:

1. **Brainstorm assets.** List all the potential branding elements you've come up with in steps 1 and 2 without filtering.

2. **Identify a theme.** Look for a common thread among your assets, like "trash" for the Danbury Trashers or "detective board" for the Dark Horse agency.

3. **Select a few assets.** Choose elements that:

   - Form a unique combination in your industry
   - Excite you and your team (maybe even make you a bit nervous)
   - Push boundaries while remaining recognizable in your category

My chosen theme is: _____

My selected **assets** are:

1. _____
2. _____
3. _____

The Doubts: "I'm Not Creative!"

"I'm not an artist or designer. How can I develop my brand assets?"

I'm no artist either, but you'd be surprised how far you can go if you don't listen too much to the voice in your head. If you have some ideas but can't flesh them out or put them on paper, you can work with service providers who'd be happy to help you out. Working with experts can also be a huge shortcut through all the indecision.

In other words, don't be afraid to outsource because all the work you've done so far can be used as a great brief to send to folks to help.

"I'm not creative. I can't come up with good ideas."

You might not think of yourself as creative. But everyone *can* become more creative by working on it. It's about feeding your brain with interesting stuff, asking yourself silly questions, reading books that have nothing to do with your field, following people you disagree with . . . and just trying stuff.

"Where can I find inspiration?"

Engage with high-quality content such as books, music, and art to stimulate your creativity. Also, try to break out of your bubble—for example, I like to browse subreddits where folks I tend to disagree with hang out. Use your interests to your advantage and learn from what others are doing in your field.

"How can I get inspired by others without feeling like I'm stealing their work?"

It's easy to feel like a creative thief, but remember: nothing is *truly* original. Every idea is a remix, so give yourself permission to be inspired by others.

A little story to illustrate my point:

Singer-songwriter Ed Sheeran was on trial recently for potential copyright infringement.[57] The case boiled down to a chord sequence that he allegedly stole from an obscure 1973 song. Sheeran argued, "Yes, it's a chord sequence you hear in successful songs, but if you say a song from 1973 owns it, then what about all the songs that came before?" His team found similar melodies in songs dating back to the 1700s. Their point? Songs should never be copied, of course, but you simply cannot copyright every single element of a song—like a chord progression.

---

57 Hayleigh Bosher. 2023. "In the Courts: Ed Sheeran Succeeds in Music Copyright Infringement Case, but It's Not over Yet . . ." *WIPO*. https://www.wipo.int /wipo_magazine_digital/en/2023/article_0027.html.

The same goes for standing the f*ck out. All the components—the words, colors, shapes, concepts, hooks—they've all been used before. But that doesn't mean we can't use them. It's how we remix, combine, and play with them that makes the difference.

The Recap: Don't Taste Like Water

Your branding shouldn't taste like water—it needs to be distinctive enough to cut through the noise. Forget chasing preexisting meanings; instead, focus on creating meaning-free **assets** that tickle different parts of the brain.

Let's recap the key takeaways:

- **Pay attention to what others notice.** What quirky details about you or your brand do people comment on? Amplify those.

- **Explore the negative space.** What branding elements are your competitors overlooking? That's where you'll find your unique edge.

- **List all potential assets and pick one or two.** Choose a theme and select **assets** that form a unique combination, excite you, and push boundaries without being confusing.

- **Don't be afraid to outsource.** If you have ideas but lack design skills, collaborate with a designer to bring your vision to life.

- **Feed your creativity.** Engage with diverse content, ask yourself silly questions, and step outside your comfort zone to spark fresh ideas.

The Recap: Distinctive Brand

A **distinctive brand** helps you to get noticed for all the right reasons *without* alienating your audience or sacrificing relationships. In this stage, we uncovered four additional elements: **monster, POV, spices,** and **assets,** pictured in the introduction to Stage 3 and again here.

Figure S3.1. The four additional insights used to craft a distinctive brand.

Let's recap the key takeaways from this stage:

• **Don't blame the people in your audience for their struggles.** Instead, identify the real **monster** holding them back and frame your brand as the solution to fight it.

• **Signal to the folks in your segment that you're there to protect them with a POV.** Insert it everywhere you can—and find 1,000 ways to share it.

• **Talk is cheap.** Spice it up! Your actions must match your words to prove you're not like the others.

• **Don't taste like water.** Create meaning-free **assets** that tickle different parts of your **segment's** brain.

To wrap things up, let's put together a distinctive brand kit that gets you noticed.

DISTINCTIVE BRAND KIT

Message: What to say

Build rapport by naming the **monster**. Share your **POV** to show how it's causing **ignored struggle(s)**. Tease the **job** and how life looks with the **monster** defeated. Introduce the **category** and the features.

Don't treat this narrative as a way to *sell*; think of it as a way to *relate*. Read it out loud and make changes until it doesn't feel weird.

Behavior: What to do

Spice: too _____

- Action: _____
- Inaction: _____
- Example: _____

Branding: What to feel

Assets:

- Color(s): _____
- Shape(s): _____
- A face: _____
- A sound: _____
- A short phrase: _____

STAGE 4

Continuous Reach

December 14, 2012

"Hi Louis, we're always on the lookout for enthusiastic digital marketers. Fancy a chat sometime?"

Fucking finally.

After investing the little savings I had in a 12-week professional diploma in digital marketing, after working in the car industry forever (OK, three years), after weeks of job hunting, I am finally getting somewhere.

The CEO of an up-and-coming Irish start-up got in touch with me! And he genuinely seemed interested in my profile after sending a connection request on this new social network called LinkedIn.

Sometime in January 2013

I got the job! It was my *dream* to work in marketing.

Enter the "digital marketing enthusiast" version of me. I was a walking *Larousse* dictionary of marketing jargon with exactly *zero* real-world experience—yet I thought I knew it all. For example, I thought I knew exactly what makes customers loyal. Loyalty programs are key to increasing revenue. Eighty percent of revenue comes from twenty percent of customers. Growing a business means making sure to turn customers into raving fans. It's just common sense.

Remember, I talked about this experience in Chapter 7. We sold bulk SMS solutions to local shops like butchers and beauty salons. One of our arguments was that SMS builds loyalty.

I was fully on board with it; it made total sense.

It's only *years* later, after I left and failed at my first marketing agency, that I discovered the truth. Pretty much everything I thought I knew about loyalty marketing was *demonstrably* wrong.[58] Turns out:

- **It's 60 percent—not 80 percent—of revenue that comes from 20 percent of customers.** A big chunk of revenue tends to come from light buyers.[59] Meaning around 40 percent of revenue comes from folks who very, very rarely buy from the brand.

- **Loyalty programs have a *very weak* effect on sales.** That's because they appeal to customers who already purchase more frequently than the average.

- **There's no evidence to back up customers falling in love with brands.** (Yes, yes, even Apple.)

To be clear, I'm *not* saying to forget about making your current customers happy so they rave about you. Sure, that's important. But here's the kicker: a lot of the time, folks leave for reasons totally out of your hands—like moving to another city or changing jobs.

What to do?

Continuously reach as many of the right people as possible when it's most relevant to them (within your means). That nonstop activity constantly

58 I realized I knew nothing thanks to the work of Wiemer Snijders, Byron Sharp, and other mar-keters who rely on science and fact— instead of opinion— to make marketers a bit less hated.

59 Learn more about light buyers and which customers matter most in Chapter 4 of Byron Sharp's book, *How Brands Grow: What Marketers Don't Know.* Oxford University Press, 2010.

puts you in front of the people in your **segment** so they see you all the time, think about you all the time, and remember you when the time is right for them to buy.

In this stage, you will uncover the final three elements: **triggers, channels, and offers.** (See Figure S4.1.)

Figure S4.1. The last three insights used to reach people.

Then you'll use those final elements to put together a **plan for continuous reach.** The cool kids call this a go-to-market (GTM) strategy.

12

The Triggers

Finding people with **struggles** that you can solve better than **alternatives** is *not* enough to stand the f*ck out. You need something else.

If you've ever watched the Looney Tunes cartoons, you've probably seen Wile E. Coyote trying to blow Road Runner to smithereens with some explosive trinitrotoluene (TNT). Wile E. Coyote isn't the only one trying to set off TNT, as shown in Figure 12.1.

Figure 12.1. Roger the Rooster, poised and ready.

TNT is an interesting compound.

It was initially used as a yellow dye. It took 30 years to discover its explosive properties because it's an extremely stable compound. It can be safely poured into shells, it doesn't interact with water, and it can be shaken vigorously without exploding.

However, if triggered by a small starter explosive, it will unleash a boom symphony that would leave Michael Bay speechless.

The Problem: We Behave Just Like TNT

Turns out, people behave just like TNT. They don't *take action* unless *something else* causes them to. This is often overlooked, yet I would argue it is the most important piece of information you can collect about your **segment**.

This *something* else refers to triggers. They are the events or situations that motivate people to make progress toward their goals and seek solutions to their problems.

I've noticed this concept doesn't come naturally to folks—yes, even seasoned marketers. They get stuck on "pain points," which don't explain what makes people act. And that's your edge, especially as an underdog going up against big corporations. While they're busy analyzing abstract pain, you can connect with the real, relatable **triggers** that get people moving.

You can have a truly painful lower back (the **struggle** in this case) for more than a decade *without* doing anything about it. It's only when you learn that your grandkids are coming over to visit next month (the **trigger** event) that you finally book an appointment with a physio so you can play in the park together (the **job**).

The Solution: The Three Things People Need to Act

You need three things for people to *do* something:

1. A **job** (*check*)

2. At least one **struggle** (*check*)

And . . .

3. At least one **trigger**

Just because you have identified a segment with a painful struggle doesn't mean you're done. You need to really think about the shifting context—the **trigger(s)** that make people say, "I need to make progress right now."

There are three characteristics of good **triggers**:

- **They are event-based.** They are *specific* moments in time and not vague pain points.

- **They are not always tied to a specific decision.** They can occur days, months, even years beforehand, or they could happen just seconds before it.

- **They are diverse.** They can be either biological (like being hungry), social (like seeing someone using a product), emotional[60] (like feeling angry), or situational[61] (like moving to a new house).

Example:

Let's go back to the toilet scent packet example to illustrate this fundamental concept.

Once again, I will forage for some insights to show you real, juicy **triggers** "in the wild." I've picked three product reviews that mention events or situations that motivated customers to buy the product. Can you find the **triggers**?

- "This product will work wonderfully for my upcoming cruise . . . it smells so nice and seems to work great!"

---

60 Our mood influences our behavior, which is called the "affect heuristic." "Affect heuristic." Wikipedia. https://en.wikipedia.org/wiki/Affect_heuristic.

61 Major life events trigger more purchases and brand switching. Research shows brand switching increases from 8 percent to 21 percent during these events. Richard Shotton. *The Choice Factory: 25 Behavioural Biases That Influence What We Buy.* Harriman House, 2018.

- "Easy to use! Going to travel soon and it will be super handy in small spaces."

- "I love these! I mostly use them when visiting someone's house, and it does what it's supposed to: mask the odor. There may be a slight citrusy scent left in the air, but it's so subtle and at least it's eliminating the unpleasant odor."

What specific events or situations can you find? What got customers moving?

Table 12.1 explains the **triggers** I found from the reviews.

Table 12.1. Breaking Down Toilet Packet's Triggers

Quotes	Explanation
"For my upcoming cruise."	This customer has probably booked a cruise with family or friends, which made her think about the toilet situation and start looking at a way to mask bathroom odors.
"Going to travel soon."	A similar event as the previous, where the customer is going on a trip soon, which led the customer to look at ways to get the **job** done
"When visiting someone's house."	Another specific moment in time mentioned by a customer who associates this product with visiting someone's house

OK, now let's up the ante a little bit by making sure we understand the difference between a **struggle** and a **trigger**. This is critical for the little guys that we are because big multinationals can afford to be *everywhere*, but we can't. We have to be laser-focused.

Solving the right struggles helps us offer something meaningful to the people in our audience, which gives them a compelling reason to choose us over others. **Understanding their triggers allows us to be present in the proper** *context*—**like the right** *moment* **or** *place*—**in a** *relatable* **way,** which gives us another advantage to stand the f*ck out.

Let's play a little game in Table 12.2.

Table 12.2. Trigger or Struggle?

Situation	Trigger or Struggle?	Why?
You are feeling self-conscious about your appearance.	Struggle	This is likely an ongoing feeling, not a specific event.
You've been invited to a wedding this summer, so you want to look your best.	**Trigger**	It's a specific event that creates a deadline and a strong motivator to take action.
You're reading an article about the unusual origins and production process of civet poop coffee.	**Trigger**	It's not a specific problem to solve, but it's a specific event that might lead to a purchase someday.
You're bored with your current coffee routine.	Struggle	You may have been bored with it for years without taking any action.
A friend invites you to watch the ice hockey playoffs at a local sports bar.	**Trigger**	It's a social invitation, a specific point in time.
You're finding that the ice hockey game has become boring to watch.	Struggle	Nothing indicates that an action would be taken, so it's not a **trigger**.

Situation	Trigger or Struggle?	Why?
You're a freelance marketer who wants to get more high-quality leads.	Struggle	Which freelance marketer does *not* want to get more high-quality leads? This is probably an ongoing problem, not a **trigger** event.
You've just received an email from your best client saying, "We're moving forward with an in-house team and don't need your services anymore."	**Trigger**	This specific moment in time is likely to prompt you to act to compensate for the lost income.

Trigger Structure

To understand triggers and avoid overlooking any crucial detail, I find it really helpful to dissect them into their fundamental contextual elements. Why? Because being present in the right context is our best chance to relate with our **segment**.

To be clear, it's not necessary to have *every* contextual element for each **trigger**. Only use the ones that are relevant; don't feel obligated to force them otherwise. Table 12.3 shows examples of **triggers** with their context attached.

Table 12.3. Structuring Triggers with Context

Triggers	When is it happening?	Where is it happening?	With whom is it happening?	With what is it happening?
Toilet packet: Someone has just booked a holiday with family or friends, which made the person think about the toilet situation.		At home	With her friends	With her computer in front of her

Triggers	When is it happening?	Where is it happening?	With whom is it happening?	With what is it happening?
LatinUs Beauty: My birthday is coming up; we have a big night out planned with the girls; I better sort my hair out.	A few weeks before my birthday, every year		With the girls	With a group chat
PTDC online training: A gym client moves to another city/country and wants to keep working with the PTDC.	When a client announces he's moving	At the gym	With the gym client	
East Forged cold brew tea: It's the end of the day and I'm thinking about treating myself.	In the evening, any day of the week	On the way back from work, or after arriving at home	On my own or with my partner	In the car
Freelance marketer: You've just received an email from your best client saying, "We're moving forward with an in-house team and don't need your services anymore."	When working on my laptop	At home or at a coworking space	Alone	

Next let's identify the right **triggers**.

The Plan: How to Find Your Triggers

Step 1. Find the Catalysts

This method relies on looking at what Jobs to Be Done expert Alan Klement calls *catalysts*.[62] They're essentially a different way to discover trigger events. Don't worry too much about the name; it's just a different way to find events that might make someone use your product or service. Check out Table 12.4 for examples.

Table 12.4. Catalysts

Catalyst Type	Description	Example
Anticipated event	Expecting that something will happen	"My friend's quinceañera is coming up, and I want my hair to look amazing."
Unexpected event	Something that has happened that caught you by surprise	"My main client just dropped me! I need to find new clients quickly."
Repeated event	Something that has happened in the past has happened again.	"Tax season is coming up and I need help with my bookkeeping."
Advertisement	Promotional content intended to inform consumers of a product and/or persuade them to use it	"I saw this post about a toilet scent packet on Instagram."
Word of mouth	Firsthand information gained from someone	"My friend told me their local ice hockey team are savages; I need to go see that."
Observed use	Seeing someone using something that was previously unknown to you	"This podcaster's voice sounds so deep. I wonder which microphone they're using."

---

62   Alan Klement. 2019. "The Jobs to Be Done Data Model." JTBD.info. https://jtbd.info/the-jobs-to-be-done-data-model-b270f6fc445.

Catalyst Type	Description	Example
Positive experience with product	Consumption of a product has made the consumer believe progress is likely.	"I've just bought a stylish robe—and now I must get things that go with it."
Negative experience with product	Consumption of a product has made the consumer believe progress is not likely.	"My new bird feeder just got stolen by crows; I need to get something that they can't steal." (True story)

Example:

Remember my failed attempt at running a marketing agency in Dublin (Chapter 7)? It's still an experience I think about often, and I want to exorcize my demons, so let's use it as an example to explain this concept.

To give you a clearer picture of **triggers** in action, I dug through old client files and share examples in Table 12.5.

Table 12.5. Triggers for My Old Agency, Based on Real Clients

Clients	Triggers	Catalyst Type
Online business selling motor racing decals	From my notes: "They currently receive an average of 40,000 visitors a month and get an average of 80 orders weekly. They would like to reach at least 200 orders weekly by the end of 2017. They want guidance on improving their conversion rates to reach this objective."	**Expected event—** new target
Software company based in Dublin	The French website conversion rate was lower than the American equivalent—and they wanted to understand why.	**Unexpected event—** poor performance

Clients	Triggers	Catalyst Type
Local provider of under-stairs storage solutions	The owner called me after seeing me speak at a local marketing conference.	Advertisement—event
Private school for professional career qualifications	The new academic year leads to a rethinking of their strategy.	Repeated event—new academic year

It's funny; it's nearly been 10 years, but the **triggers** in this table are as relevant now as they were back then.

TAKE ACTION

Catalysts give you a different way to look at the **trigger** events you identified during **insight foraging**. For each type of catalyst, look at your research—and use your intuition—to see if you can spot some:

- Anticipated event
    - _____
    - _____
    - _____

- Unexpected event
    - _____
    - _____
    - _____

- Repeated event
    - _____
    - _____
    - _____

- Advertisement
  - _____
  - _____
  - _____

- Word of mouth
  - _____
  - _____
  - _____

- Observed use
  - _____
  - _____
  - _____

- Positive experience with product
  - _____
  - _____

- Negative experience with product
  - _____
  - _____

Step 2. Investigate the Status Shift

This technique assumes people are driven by a desire for status, even if they don't realize it. We want to look for subtle clues that reveal how people try to elevate their status—even if you won't hear them admit it directly. We humans are social creatures, constantly navigating a complex web of hierarchies and relationships (with family, with friends, at work, with strangers . . .). Our place in this web—our status—is what makes us act. Changes in this status, or the threat of such changes, can be powerful **triggers**.

People often prioritize *status* over *truth* (as depicted in Figure 12.2), but this isn't something that marketing teams in big corporations tend to think about much.

Figure 12.2. Status over truth

First, think about the status markers for the people in your segment. What are the symbols, achievements, or possessions that signify status? What does "high status" look like in their world? What about "low status"?

Let's go back to my failed agency experience. I was mostly dealing with local business owners who wanted to grow—nothing really surprising here. Their status markers tend to be around things like year-on-year growth, number of employees, being featured in local media, getting an award, and so on.

Then you could think about what could cause a *shift* in status. You'd take the status markers you have identified and ask yourself what changes could happen that would threaten or impact each marker. For the clients of my failed agency, let's look at what may threaten or elevate each status marker.

Year-on-year growth:

- **Threat.** Growth projected isn't as high as last year. A new competitor enters the market and is gaining traction.

- **Elevation.** Growth surpasses all previous years. Win a major contract that significantly boosts revenue.

Number of employees:

- **Threat.** A competitor's number of recent hires suggests the competitor is growing, putting pressure on your business, especially given your current financial constraints.

- **Elevation.** The business goes on a hiring spree to keep up with demand.

Getting an award:

- **Threat.** A competitor wins an industry award. The business is nominated but doesn't win, leading to a perception of "second best."

- **Elevation.** The business wins a prestigious national award. The award is highly recognized within its industry and gives the business the confidence to invest in growth.

It's clear that those business owners are unlikely to admit that any of those status shifts are why they took action—especially the negative ones. This is why using this technique is super helpful to uncover deeply rooted motivations.

TAKE ACTION

People are driven by status, even if they don't admit it. This exercise helps you uncover those hidden motivations. Here's what to do:

1. **Identify status markers.** What symbols, achievements, or possessions signify high and low status for your **segment**?

2. **Pay attention to status shifts.** For each status marker, think about potential events or changes that could:

   ◦ Lower their status (e.g., competitor gains traction).

   ◦ Increase their status (e.g., win a prestigious award).

Step 3. Identify the Most Potent Triggers

You may have uncovered a truckload of specific events that made your segment act. Now we must select the ones that have the biggest potential. To do this, you want to list all the **trigger** events you've identified in Stage 1 as well as the new ones you may have found in this chapter.

Then have a quick read through each and see if you can find ways to merge them in a set of coherent **triggers**, particularly if the same type is appearing time and time again. Table 12.6 gathers the potential **triggers** I've discovered for my failed marketing agency and labels them based on emerging themes.

Table 12.6. Labeling Triggers for My Failed Marketing Agency

Triggers	Labels
"They currently receive an average of 40,000 visitors a month and get an average of 80 orders a week. They would like to reach at least 200 orders weekly by the end of 2017. They want guidance on improving their conversion rates to reach this objective."	Internal goals, website conversions
The French website conversion rate was lower than the American equivalent—and they wanted to understand why.	Internal goals, website conversions
The owner called me after seeing me speak at a local marketing conference.	Speaking at events
The new academic year leads to a rethinking of their strategy.	New year
Growth projected isn't as high as last year.	Internal goals
A new competitor enters the market and is gaining traction.	Competitive pressure
Growth surpasses all previous years.	Internal goals
Win a major contract that significantly boosts revenue.	New sales
A direct competitor announced hiring for many new roles, which implies growth.	Competitive pressure

Triggers	Labels
The business goes on a hiring spree to keep up with demand.	Hiring, internal goals
A competitor wins an industry award.	Competitive pressure, awards
The business is nominated but doesn't win, leading to a perception of "second best."	Competitive pressure, awards
The business wins a prestigious national award. The award is highly recognized within their industry and gives them the confidence to invest in growth.	Awards, confidence

Now that we have themes emerging, we can organize the **triggers** into a more coherent list, as done in Table 12.7.

Table 12.7. Triggers for My Failed Marketing Agency

Triggers	Summary
Internal goal-oriented	New targets agreed. Meeting or missing targets
Competitive pressure	New competitor just launched. Competitor won an award or seems to be growing fast.
Seasonal	New year, new quarter
Marketing events	Seeing someone speaking at an event

TAKE ACTION

OK, it's time to identify the most powerful events that make your **segment** take action. Here's what to do:

1. **List and label.** Write down all the **trigger** events you uncovered in Stage 1 plus any new ones you've found since. Group similar triggers together and give each group a clear label.

2. **Condense/clarify.** Combine **triggers** that are super similar into a single, powerful statement. For example, "Missed sales target" and "Revenue lower than last year" could become "Failing to meet financial goals."

3. **Build your list.** Organize your final list of top **triggers**.

My top **triggers**:

1. _____

2. _____

3. _____

4. _____

5. _____

The Doubts: "It's Not Like There's a Single Event That Makes People Buy!"

"I'm having a hard time figuring out the triggers. It's not like there's a single event that makes my people act."

There is always one—either a single event or series of events. Sometimes they are cumulative and that last event is just "the final straw." Remember, without this element, there's no chemical reaction. It could be a tiny, seemingly insignificant moment in time, like seeing an ad on TV that leads you to search for the product, for example. There is *always* a **trigger**.

"The triggers I've uncovered are so inconsistent. It seems like I have hundreds of them. What should I do?"

Well, Google calls it the "messy middle"[63] for a reason; because it is a super-messy process. You might be feeling overwhelmed because you're too close to the data. Your best bet? Find the themes that all those events have in common to group them—or ask a third party to help you.

The Recap: We're Just Like TNT

People—like TNT—need a little "boom" to act. That's where **triggers** come in. These aren't vague "pain points" but specific events that make your customers say, "I need this now." While big corporations chase abstract pain, you, *mon ami*, get to connect with those relatable **triggers**.

Let's recap the key takeaways from this chapter:

- **Three things make people act:** A **job**, a **struggle**, and a **trigger**. Without a trigger, it's just a whole lotta nothing.

- **Good triggers are:**
  - Event-based (not vague)
  - Not always tied to an immediate decision
  - Biological, social, emotional, or situational

- **Unearth those triggers by:**
  - **Finding the catalysts.** Look for anticipated, unexpected, or repeated events; influences like ads, word of mouth, or observed use; and positive or negative experiences.
  - **Investigating status shifts.** Identify status markers for the people in your segment and analyze events that could threaten or elevate their status.

---

63 Alistair Rennie and Jonny Protheroe. "Navigating Purchase Behavior & Decision-Making." 2020. *Think with Google.* https://www.thinkwithgoogle.com/consumer-insights/consumer-journey/navigating-purchase-behavior-and-decision-making/.

- **Find the most potent triggers.** Group similar **triggers** together, condense them into powerful statements, and prioritize the most impactful ones.

13

The Channels

Imagine you've been hired by a major hospital with thousands of staff. Your mission is simple: you have six months to improve the staff members' health by encouraging them to drink more water.

What do you do?

When I started to think about the problem, I thought about activities like:

- Running a hospital-wide challenge where everyone competes against each other
- Sending a series of 10 emails about the health benefits of water versus soda
- Organizing a seminar with world-renowned dietitians
- Setting up a free health clinic to check on their health

In short, I was probably going to try to *convince* the nurses, doctors, technicians, and therapists to change their minds and habits. If you had similar ideas, I have some bad news for you. Your tenure as a consultant is going to be short-lived.

> That's because *communicating* about the benefits of water is unlikely to make a sizable impact—because people have this weird tendency to do the opposite of what someone wants them to do.[64]

So, what's the solution?

It comes from a real story mentioned in the book *Atomic Habits* by James Clear: Anne Thorndike, a primary care physician at Massachusetts General Hospital in Boston, was tasked with this exact challenge.

She did something super simple and . . . the impact?

Soda sales declined by 11 percent, while water sales increased by 26 percent.

The Problem: Marketing Isn't Communications

Here's the only thing Anne did: **she increased the number of places where water was available in the cafeteria, without communicating about it.**

That's it. *C'est tout!*

You see, *marketing* has become synonymous with *communications*. Communicating that our product is the best. Communicating that customers should pick us and not the competition. Communicating that we can be trusted.

Marketing bad boy Mark Ritson calls it "communification."[65] In his words, it's marketers who "focus on one small, relatively unimportant subset of marketing tactics—communications—for all their efforts."

Since Anne did *not* communicate about this change, something else must be at play.

---

64 Christina Steindl, Eva Jonas, Sandra Sittenthaler, Eva Traut-Mattausch, and Jeff Greenberg. "Understanding Psychological Reactance: New Developments and Findings." *Zeitschrift Fur Psychologie* 223, no. 4 (2015): 205–214. https://doi.org/10.1027/2151-2604/a000222.

65 This is one of his four marketing pet peeves. The other three are mortification (everything is dead), tactification (no time for strategy), and digitization (obsession with digital). "What Ails Marketing?" In Wiemer Snijders, Ed. *Eat Your Greens: Fact-Based Thinking to Improve Your Brand's Health. Matador*, 2018.

The Solution: You Don't Always Need to Convince People

People often choose products not because of what they are, but because of where they are.

— JAMES CLEAR

This experiment shows that **we don't always need to obsess over what we're going to say to convince people to give us a go; we *just* need to be in the right place.**

This **"right place" is the channel. It's a means of meeting potential customers in the context where they experience their triggers, compare alternatives, and can easily find/buy[66] the category.** While your competitors are busy blasting generic messages into the void (aka "communificating"), you've got a golden opportunity.

> Just by showing up in those places—being present and accessible—you can become a familiar face long *before* they even think about opening their wallets.

Let's debunk some misconceptions I often come across.

A **channel** is:

- **Not always "on the internet."** We're not stuck living in an ergonomic pod, hooked by a neural implant as our only link to civilization (yet); we do get out in the real world sometimes.

- **Not the same thing as an "influencer."** For example, if your customers buy your goat yoga classes because they saw a post on Instagram about it, the author of the post is the influencer (the *who*) and the Instagram post would be the specific **channel** (the *where*).

---

66 Learn more about the three main components of physical availability in Chapter 12 of Byron Sharp's book, *How Brands Grow: What Marketers Don't Know.* Oxford University Press, 2010.

- **Meant to be specific.** For example, "social media" is not a **channel**. In fact, it's so wide, you can almost see it from space. That's because it's not information you can take and act on. Like, which social network? Twitter or FeetFinder? How are you going to get in front of them? Using ads or organically?

There might be more than this, but not that many. I'm also blending traditional "communication" versus distribution **channels** because the line is blurred—you can buy directly from email, for example. I've added the most common ones in Table 13.1.

Table 13.1. Types of Channels

Channel Type	Description	Examples
Direct distribution	Selling things directly to people	**Toilet packet:** Selling directly on the company's website
Direct mail	Sending letters and fly-ers to people's mailboxes	**At my first marketing job,** we posted a mini-magazine with the latest news about mobile marketing to our clients.
Email	Sending messages to people's email inboxes	**Stand The F*ck Out:** I send emails to my subscribers every weekday (Mon–Fri).
Event	Being present during in-person gatherings	**East Forged cold brew tea:** Meeting customers in large makers markets (more than 10,000 attendees)
Indirect distribution	Selling things through someone else	**LatinUs Beauty shampoo:** Selling the products through Amazon Marketplace
Outdoor	Appearing in public places	**Demo Diva:** Placing signs in empty lots that just got demolished
Partnership	Partnering up with peo-ple with an audience	**Everyone Hates Marketers podcast:** Inviting guests on my podcast in exchange for their wisdom and clout
Podcast	Reaching people through audio shows	**Online fitness trainer:** Jonathan Good-man guesting on other podcasts

Channel Type	Description	Examples
Print	Appearing in newspapers and magazines	**Toilet packet:** Getting featured in in-flight magazines
Radio	Reaching people through broadcasted radio	Getting interviewed on local radio
Search	Appearing in online search results	**All-in-one tool for PDFs:** Appearing in search results for use cases like "compress PDF" or "PDF to Excel"
Social	Using social media platforms	**Shanty Biscuits:** Posting parody videos on Instagram during Covid
TV	Appearing on television	Brands sponsoring the weather
Video	Appearing in online videos	**Shampoo for Latinas:** Producing a telenovela—Lu: The Power of Us—to appear on YouTube

You can reach the people in your audience through owned **channels** (they've opted in), paid **channels** (you're paying for access), or earned **channels** (you're getting attention organically).

How to Structure Channels

To make sure you have the best chance of identifying places where potential customers experience their **triggers**, compare **alternatives**, and buy the **category**, use the structure in Table 13.2.

Table 13.2. Channel Structure

	Definition	Question to Answer
Name	The specific **channel** you'll use	What should we call it so it's easy to understand?

	Definition	Question to Answer
Type	See Table 13.1 for a full list.	What type of **channel** is it?
Objective	The primary focus	What's the main objective: sales activation (generating sales) or brand-building (becoming top-of-mind)?
Reach	How you'll reach your **segment**	Will you rely on paid promotion, organic efforts, or a combination?
Context	Additional details for clarity	What additional information can you give to make it actionable?

By carefully considering these elements, you can create a channel strategy that puts you in front of the right people at the right time, maximizing your chances of standing the f*ck out.

Example:

When the founders of LatinUs Beauty planned their launch, they identified a medium that Latinas in particular liked: telenovelas. They cast big-name Spanish-speaking actors—Sofia Castro, Victoria Ruffo, and Marlene Favela—with a story following three generations of women as they live between Mexico and the United States while building a hair care business.[67] See Table 13.3.

Table 13.3. LatinUs Beauty Trailer

	Lu: The Power of Us **Telenovela Trailer**
Type	Video
Objective	Brand-building (becoming top-of-mind)
Reach	Paid

---

67 *Lu: The Power of US—Conoce a Lu.* 2021. YouTube. https://www.youtube.com/watch?v=DY28mjhRXqQ.

	Lu: The Power of Us **Telenovela Trailer**
Context	Trailer shared on YouTube via paid ads

Example:

Going back to my failed marketing agency, I spent €6,000 to speak at four conferences in one year.[68] Nobody knew me, so I used a shortcut. I contacted every marketing conference organizer in Ireland, hoping to get invited. When I realized that I wouldn't be able to speak with my current profile, I chose the most accessible option: paying for it. See Table 13.4.

Table 13.4. Paying to Speak as a Channel

	Paying to Speak at Irish Conferences
Type	Event
Objective	Sales activation (generating sales)
Reach	Paid
Context	Getting a speaking spot when sponsoring local, marketing-centric conferences

Example:

Remember the field notes I shared from East Forged cold brew tea in Chapter 3? The East Forged people set up shop at massive makers markets (three-day events with over 10,000 attendees). In total, they attended over 36 markets and interacted with over 5,000 customers. See Table 13.5.

---

68 Louis Grenier. 2016. "Why I Paid to Speak at Conferences." *Slices Consulting Blog.* https://web. archive.org /web/20171114180418/http:// slicesconsulting.com/paid-speak-conferences/.

Table 13.5. Setting Up Shop at Markets

	Paying to Exhibit at Markets
Type	Event
Objective	Sales activation (generating sales)
Reach	Paid
Context	Securing an exhibition stand to talk directly to visitors and sell their products

The Plan: Three Steps to Take to Uncover Channels

Step 1. Be Where People Experience Their Triggers

This technique taps into your uncovered triggers to pinpoint the perfect places to connect with your segment. It's my favorite way to identify the right **channels** because it flips the script: you're forced to see things through your customers' eyes and understand how they *actually* buy stuff.

> In other words, this *isn't* about slapping your message onto some random marketing channel because your boss thinks it's *très très chic.*

Here's how it works.

Start with the triggers you uncovered in the last chapter. Break each **trigger** down into its contextual components: when, *where, with whom,* and *with what.* Then for each component determine which **channels** would put you directly in front of your ideal customers as they experience these **triggers.**

Your goal is to build associations between the buying **triggers** and your brand. **It feels a bit like magic honestly, because it feels like your campaign and the way you're going to reach people is unfolding before your eyes. It becomes so obvious, it's fucking great.**

Example:

Say we go back to the toilet scent packet example and take one of the potent **triggers** we've found to get started: *someone has just booked a holiday with family or friends, which made the person think about the toilet situation.*

Before I share what this particular **trigger** made me think about in terms of **channels**, I really invite you to have a think yourself first. I want to show you how simple it is to use this method.

So ask yourself:

How can you be present around the time when this specific **trigger** happens?

I'll wait on the other page.

Done?

Cool.

Where did your mind go? Finding a way to be featured on digital travel websites? Maybe partnering up with travel agents? Writing travel-centric articles that relate to the toilet situation problem? All of the above?

But then what happens if we were to intersect that **trigger** with the core **segment** we've identified, as shown in Figure 13.1? Folks with digestive issues, who are self-conscious about it, who can afford a holiday abroad?

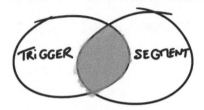

Figure 13.1. Intersection of trigger and segment.

Because this is where the magic really happens. It can be very overwhelming to think about all the possible ways to get in front of the right people at the right time. Still, if you start with the cross-section—where each **trigger** and **segment** intersect—you will naturally drill down into precise **channels**, as shown in Figure 13.2.

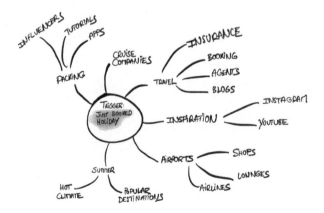

Figure 13.2. Mind map of "just-booked holiday" channels.

By now, I hope you can sense the power of this technique. I'm just scratching the surface here, but I'm sure you can see how powerful breaking down each **trigger** is. For example, we could partner with travel influencers (partnership) who talk about packing or share destination ideas—starting with those who openly talk about going abroad when suffering from digestive issues (see Table 13.6). Or we could look into selling our toilet scent packet in airports (indirect distribution).

Table 13.6. "Just-Booked Holiday" Channels

Context	Trigger: just booked a holiday
When	Summer (hot climate, popular destinations)
Where	Airports (shops, lounges, airlines) Cruises
With whom	Travel agents Friends Family
With what	Travel inspiration (Instagram, YouTube) Packing (influencers, tutorials, apps) Travel insurance

Example:

Let's take another look at my failed marketing agency and the people I sought to serve: local e-commerce business owners. One of their **triggers** was seasonal: it's a new year or quarter, and new targets need to be reached. I'm breaking them down in Table 13.7.

Table 13.7. "New Quarter/Year" Channels

Context	Trigger: New Year, New Quarter
When	A few weeks before the new year

Context	Trigger: New Year, New Quarter
Where	Events and conferences (chamber of commerce, start-up accelerators, marketing or industry-specific events) Lurking online, in particular on LinkedIn
With whom	Fellow business owners Senior team members Freelancers and agencies they're already working with Accountant, financial advisor
With what	Financial reports in Excel

If I could go back in time, I'd probably double down on being present at every relevant event in and around Dublin, especially when new year planning is underway. I wouldn't obsess over being a keynote speaker; instead, I would focus on talking to and learning from as many e-commerce business owners as possible.

TAKE ACTION

Identify the best **channels** to reach your audience by analyzing their **triggers**.

Here's what to do:

1. **List the triggers you uncovered in Chapter 12 and break them down into these components:**
   - When
   - Where
   - With whom
   - With what

2. **For each component, brainstorm channels** to put you in front of your ideal customers as they experience these triggers.

3. **Refine your channel ideas** by considering the intersection of each trigger with your core segment.

Step 2. Become the Trigger

This technique relies on engineering moments that would trigger folks to action. Instead of being present while folks experience triggers, this technique allows us to be proactive to accelerate or even create a buying moment.

We all know word of mouth is marketing gold. But you can engineer it. How? By giving people stories worth sharing. Not just testimonials, but conversation-worthy stories that spread organically, even if the listener isn't *actively* looking for your stuff.

In *Talk Triggers*,[69] Daniel Lemin and Jay Baer share five types of stories that get people talking. I've added them to Table 13.8.

---

69 Jay Baer and Daniel Lemin. Talk Triggers: *The Complete Guide to Creating Customers with Word of Mouth*. Portfolio, 2019.

Table 13.8. Talk Triggers

Talk Triggers	What It Is	Example
Empathy	Showing that you care, for real	Pet food retailer Chewy routinely sends flowers after a customer's pet passes away.
Usefulness	Being of service when folks need it most	**Shanty Biscuit** shared fun, light-hearted content at the height of Covid when the atmosphere was doom and gloom.
Generosity	Giving, giving, giving, without expecting anything in return	**The PTDC online fitness training**'s 100 percent free online training software is super generous and triggers users to talk about it to other trainers.
Speed	Delivering results much faster than expected	A few months ago, I requested a callback from my payment provider Stripe. Within 5 seconds—oui, 5 seconds—a friendly agent called me back and fixed the issue while we were on the phone.
Attitude	Being a nice human	**The people at LatinUs Beauty shampoo** reach out personally to early customers to learn about their experience.

The best way to identify a story worth sharing is to look back at the insights you've gathered throughout this book. What small things do people notice? What would your **spices** dictate?

Other ways to become the **trigger**, which are in your control:

- **Social proof.** How can you ensure that more people see how your product/service affects people?

- **Usage.** How can you make your product/service more visible so other people see your customers using it? Maybe change the packaging or the way people use it online?

- **Ads.** When they see your ad, they think of you and might buy immediately.

TAKE ACTION

Create a story that triggers word of mouth.

Here's what to do:

1. **Review Table 13.8.** Look at the five types of **talk triggers:** empathy, usefulness, generosity, speed, and attitude.

2. **Choose one trigger type.**

3. **Brainstorm a simple, unexpected story** based on your chosen trigger type. Use these prompts:

   ○ What little things do your customers notice?

   ○ How can you show you give a shit?

   ○ What can you offer that's super useful or generous?

   ○ How can you surprise people with speed or a positive attitude?

4. **Find ways to implement your story idea** in your business operations.

My story idea is: _____

How I'll make it visible: _____

Step 3. Select Your Channels

The last step is to pick the **channels** that'll give you the highest chance of reaching the people in your **segment** in the context where they experience their **triggers**, compare **alternatives**, and can easily find/buy the **category**. I advise using the following two criteria to narrow down your list.

Penetration: how many people can you reach via this channel?

Forget about finding that mythical "blue ocean"[70] where you're the only fish swimming. It's a mirage. Instead, focus on **channels** with the most people you can reach. Why? Because **channels** that attract bigger numbers will be used more often and for longer than smaller ones.[71]

How to gauge penetration? First, identify the right metrics. For online **channels**, look into daily active users (DAU). For physical distribution, look for foot traffic or market share. Then gather data from any sources you can find—but don't expect to find perfect sources that will give you the exact answer you're looking for. Finally, estimate the overall penetration by comparing the **channel's** size with your **segment's** size.

Joy: how much do you like this channel?

Standing the f*ck out isn't a sprint; it's a marathon. Choose places where you can go the distance without burning out. A good way to do this is to focus on **channels** that (1) you're familiar with so you don't have to learn from complete scratch and (2) you actually enjoy using or learning about.

Once you've evaluated your options, prioritize your top three **channels**. Just like in previous chapters, keep things simple by merging similar ones into common themes.

70 W. C. Kim and Renée Mauborgne. *Blue Ocean Strategy: How to Create Uncontested Market Space and Make Competition Irrelevant.* Harvard Business School Press, 2005.

71 This is called the Double Jeopardy Law. Learn more about this concept in Chapter 2 of Byron Sharp's book, *How Brands Grow: What Marketers Don't Know.* Oxford University Press, 2010.

TAKE ACTION

Select the most effective **channels** to reach your **segment**.

Here's what to do:

1. **List potential channels.** Write down all the channels you could use to reach your segment.

2. **Evaluate penetration.** For each **channel**, estimate how many people in your **segment** you can reach. Use metrics like:

   ○ Online. Daily active users (DAU)

   ○ Physical. Foot traffic or market share

3. **Assess the joy factor.** Rate each **channel** based on:

   ○ Your familiarity with it

   ○ How much you enjoy using or learning about it

4. **Merge similar channels.** If applicable, combine similar **channels** into broader themes.

My top three channels are:

1. _____

2. _____

3. _____

The Doubts: "My Budget Is Way Too Small for Any of This."

"There are so many channels to be on . . . it's overwhelming."

Don't worry about using all of them. Just pick one or two that you think will work best. Don't go overboard; you can scale later.

"My segment is way too big and the budget is way too small. There's no money to invest in any of those channels."

No money? Trade money with *time*—whether it's being active in an online community, volunteering at a trade conference where your ideal customers will be, or being invited as a guest on local radio stations in exchange for your knowledge.

See if you can refine the **segment** further so you "feel" like you know where the people in your **segment** hang out so you can reach them.

Then don't just choose places where you can "see" who's clicking on your stuff. Continuously reaching as many as possible is more affordable than you may think, while the accuracy of those measurable **channels** is, at best, debatable.

"Do I always have to try to convince people to buy stuff?"

Not always. Sometimes just being in the right place at the right time works. Make sure you show up where your segments are and show them an **offer** that's hard to say no to (which is the topic of the next chapter).

The Recap: Stop Communificating

Stuck in "communification" mode? Try to be present where your customers are instead of blasting generic messages into the void. This chapter is about understanding that sometimes the best marketing isn't about convincing; it's about being in the right place at the right time.

Let's recap the key takeaways:

- **Marketing is more than just communication.** Stop trying to convince everyone and focus on being present where your customers are.

- **You don't always need to convince people.** Sometimes just being in the right place at the right time is enough.

- **Two ways to uncover the right channels:**

- ○ **Be where people experience their triggers.** Break down your customers' **triggers** and identify **channels** that align with those moments.
- ○ **Become the trigger.** Engineer moments that trigger word of mouth by crafting shareable stories.

- **Select channels based on penetration and joy.** Penetration refers to how many people you can reach, while joy refers to how much you enjoy using the **channel**.

- **Structure your channels.** Define each channel's name, type, objective, reach, and context.

- **Don't let budget be a barrier.** Start small, focus on one or two channels, and trade time or resources if needed. Remember, reaching the right people is more important than using every **channel**.

14

The Offers

We've come to the final chapter of the book.

And yet this is where most marketing books tell you to start.

Wanna get a constant flow of customers? Wanna know the secret to online success? Wanna make your competitors say "Mon Dieu!" in awe of your success? All you need is one offer people can't refuse, one hyper-optimized funnel, and one ad using this groundbreaking approach!

That's all you need! It's that easy!

More exclamation points!!!

Fuck that.

If it were that easy, everyone would do it. But a sales funnel is not a business. Neither is an offer. Or an ad campaign. Selling stuff to people is hard. It takes time. It's meant to be hard.

My friend Billy Broas[72] was advising an online course creator making $40,000 a month solely from Facebook Ads. Sounds like a good business,

---

72 Louis Grenier and Billy Broas. 2024. "Funnels Don't Build Businesses: Here's What Does." *Everyone Hates Marketers.* https://podcast.everyonehates marketers.com/episodes/funnels- dont-build-businesses-heres-what-does.

doesn't it? $40,000 a month! Nearly half a million a year. Who wouldn't want that?

Not so fast.

> The ads inevitably stopped working after a couple of months, his revenue went to zero overnight, and he had no other option but to shut down the business. Why? **Because it had no foundations— no unique positioning, no distinctive brand, and no continuous reach—just an offer sitting on top of a house of cards (refer to my brilliant sketch in Figure 14.1) that would collapse as soon as one of the flavor-of-the-month tactics stopped working.**

Figure 14.1. Not the sturdiest foundation, to put it mildly.

"This is the big mistake I've seen well-intentioned business owners make," says Billy. "They jump from tactic to tactic, thinking the next one holds the key. Instead, they should build their business on a solid foundation of principles."

Lucky for you, since you've followed this book's methodology from the start, you *do* have those principles in place. The **offer** is the cherry on top.

The Problem: Your Segment Is Hibernating

Let's rewind for a moment to talk about the core principle behind a good offer that stands the test of time. **You see, our minds tend to operate on autopilot 95 percent of the time.[73] A compelling offer acts as a jolt to snap your segment out of it.** Daniel Kahneman, the Nobel Prize in Economics winner, proposed that our brains operate using two distinct systems, as shown in Table 14.1.

Table 14.1. System 1 Versus System 2

	System 1	System 2
Proportion of brain activity	More than 95 percent	Less than 5 percent
Speed	Fast	Slow
Effort	Low	High
Default usage	Routine decisions, habits, and simple tasks	Complex problem-solving and focused attention
Decision-making	Intuitive, impulsive	Logical, analytical

Therefore, introducing something new to your **segment's** brains is like attempting to wake up an Arctic ground squirrel buried under the snow. And let me tell you, it's not easy: its body temperature drops as low as -2.9°C without freezing—the lowest known body temperature of any mammal in hibernation.[74] Its heart rate slows from 200 beats per minute to one beat every few seconds. In short, the rodent isn't just asleep; it's almost dead.

Most people's brains operate in a state of conservation, sticking to known patterns and resisting change. We better come up with something good to wake them up from this slumber.

---

73 The concept of System 1 and System 2 thinking comes from the work of psychologist Daniel Kahneman, particularly his book *Thinking, Fast and Slow*.

74 Brian M. Barnes "Freeze Avoidance in a Mammal: Body Temperatures Below 0 Degree C in an Arctic Hibernator." *Science* 244.4912 (1989): 1593–1595.

The Solution: You've Gotta Wake Them Up

That something good is your **offer. An offer is designed to compel action from the folks in your segment—like trying software, buying a product, or downloading a movie. It's a clear, concise proposition stating how you will help them overcome their struggles and get the job done.** But it isn't some magic trick you pull out of a hat at the last minute. It's the culmination of all the hard work you've put in so far.

First, a good offer is *not* about tricking people into buying. It's about presenting a solution so irresistible, so perfectly aligned with their **struggles**, that they are more likely to say yes. For the people in your **segment**, it almost feels like you're reading their minds.

For example, Jon Goodman from the PTDC knew that personal trainers needed something other than Google Sheets to share their individual fitness programs with their clients. He spent tens of thousands to develop a coaching software solution and offers it for free. No tricks, no trials, no hidden fees. The PTDC gives the software as a free gift and hopes users will turn to the PTDC if they need support in other business areas.

Second, a good offer is generous. It shouldn't feel like a cold, hard transaction. It should feel like the people in your **segment** are getting a steal—way more than they put in. And by "put in," I don't just mean cash. I mean their precious time, the effort they'll invest, the sweat they'll pour into making it work.

For example, I hope this book feels like a generous **offer** to you, rather than a cold, hard transaction. I've distilled all my knowledge and shared uncomfortable personal stories to give you everything you need to stand the f*ck out.

Third, the best offers start small. Because you don't scare off your audience after you've worked so fucking hard to make them notice you. The goal here is to ask just enough of the customers to get your "foot in the door" without causing decision paralysis.

Here's how my coworker Fio and I at Hotjar came up with a small **offer**. During Covid, everyone was busy and working from home. Companies were doing lots of online events. We wanted to do one, too, but *differently*. Inspired by the Lightning Talk format that Hotjar's Ops team organized during our bi-yearly company meetup, we came up with the *Hotjar Lightning Talks*.[75] The offer? 5 days. 5 talks a day. 5 minutes each. Totally free. Figure 14.2 shows how this simple concept was visualized. The event brought in more than 10,000 registrations.

Figure 14.2. The concept of 5 days: 5 talks per day, 5 minutes per talk, and 5 slides per talk.

And finally, I like to think of a good offer as a gift box you can hold in your hands. Most of us work in front of a computer all day every day. So a good exercise is to imagine your offer as an actual, physical box that folks pick up, quickly scan with their eyes, and decide to buy or not—unlike a huge landing page where you can add as much as you want. Imagining it as a physical box gives you constraints. You only have room for a title, a background image, and just a few features/descriptions. That's it. It's a framework I like to use to structure an **offer** and think of it like a gift box. I call it the **BOX** framework (see Figure 14.3):

- **Basis.** What's in the box? What's the **category**? What are they getting?

- **Outcome.** Do I want what's in the box? Show them what the future could look like. They'll put the box back on the shelf if they're not into it. In other words, will it help them get the job done and avoid **struggles**?

---

75 "Lightning Talks." 2020. Hotjar. https://web.archive.org/web /20200608062933/https:// lightningtalks.hotjar.com/.

- **X-factor.** Why should I pick this box and not another one? Show them why it's the least risky choice in the context they find themselves in (aka **triggers**).

Figure 14.3. Use the BOX framework to create your offers.

The Plan: Five Steps to Build Your Offers

Step 1. Slice and Dice Your Insights

This approach involves slicing and dicing your insights into manageable, bite-sized portions to create a variety of offers. By doing so, you improve your chances of waking up the people in your **segment** from their deep sleep and being picked as an underdog.

For example, get specific when defining the **job** you help people with. Instead of saying you help businesses "increase sales," zoom in on the actionable steps within that broad goal. **What specific tasks contribute to increased sales?**

Think of it like breaking down a recipe. A recipe lists ingredients, but it also outlines the stages: chop the onions; sauté the garlic; simmer the sauce. We can apply this same principle to any **job** by breaking it down into digestible stages: define, locate, prepare, confirm, execute, monitor, modify, and conclude.

Create a matrix using these stages. On one axis, list the stages. On the other, brainstorm how you can provide solutions for each one.

Example:

Let's revisit my failed marketing agency to illustrate how this method works. More specifically, let's examine the **offer** I sent to the last big lead we got—an online business selling motor racing decals—before I burned out for good.

I had to dig into my archives to find the proposal I sent the business, and I still cringe: we were asking for a €7,200 per month retainer for 13 months . . . after meeting the people there *once*. Besides going back in time to slap myself on the back of the head with a *saucisson*, here's what I would do differently, using this method.

First, what's the **job** we could help them achieve? Looking back at my notes, they wanted guidance on improving their conversion rates to reach at least 200 orders a week by the end of 2017. So let's pick *improve conversion rates* as the **job**.

OK, next let's break this **job** down and answer the question, "What specific tasks contribute to increasing conversion rates?" Here's what I can think of:

- Make sure their website data points are correctly tracked.
- Understand what is preventing customers from buying.
- Map the buyer's journey.
- Set up surveys.
- Run an in-depth website audit.
- Identify the biggest issues.
- Come up with potential solutions to those issues.
- Turn potential solutions into website wireframes.
- Set the experiments live.
- Implement winning experiments.
- Move on to the next set of experiments.
- Send weekly reports.

That's a lot and we're only scratching the surface. We could take each task and zoom in to another level to identify the subtasks needed to get each done. But I'm going to stop at this level to show you.

Looking back, it's easy to understand why this client told me he and his team liked the proposal but felt they needed to hire more team members to have the bandwidth to make what we were proposing happen.

Instead of selling a 13-month project, what if we had developed an **offer** around the first three tasks? Maybe a personalized website audit delivered in a one-page document with specific quick fixes the client could implement tomorrow—without the need to hire anyone else?

Now that sounds less overwhelming all of a sudden. And it contributes to helping the business achieve the **job**.

Using the **BOX** framework:

- **Basis.** A 30-minute personalized video audit of your e-commerce website.

- **Outcome.**

- **20 top-priority fixes to implement on your website without hiring developers/designers.**

  - Delivered in 72 hours (or less).
  - No access to website analytics needed; we use our own methodology to identify issues around copy, structure, social proof, payments . . .

- **X-factor.** There is a money-back guarantee if you're not satisfied with this audit. No questions asked.

TAKE ACTION

Slice and dice your **insights** to create specific **offers** that address customers' needs.

Here's what to do:

1. **Identify the main job.** Choose one primary goal your client wants to achieve (e.g., improve conversion rates).

2. **Break down the job.** List 8–12 specific tasks that contribute to achieving this goal.

3. **Create a job map.**
   - Vertical axis—list the tasks you identified.
   - Horizontal axis—use *define, locate, prepare, confirm, execute, monitor, modify,* and *conclude* as your eight stages.

4. **Brainstorm solutions.** Consider what can be offered for each intersection between a task and a **job** stage.

5. **Develop focused offers.** Create smaller, more targeted **offers** based on clusters of tasks or stages in your matrix.

Step 2. Explore Cognitive Biases

This technique uses cognitive biases to find new ways to think of offers and come up with shit tons of them. With this technique, you can almost read the minds of your **segment** by tapping into thought processes we tend not to be aware of.

Example:

Once again, let's go back to my failed marketing agency to illustrate how to use this method. Table 14.2 shows a list of my favorite cognitive biases. I've added a definition for each, an example to go with each, and the ideas that came to mind for my agency.

Table 14.2. Cognitive Biases

Cognitive Biases	What It Is	Real-World Example	For My Failed Agency
Input bias and complexity bias	People often think something is better just because someone spent a lot of time/worked hard on it. And we also think things are better when they seem really complicated.	**This book:** It has been reviewed by more than 70 beta readers who left more than 5,000 reactions/comments across the three versions of the manuscript.	We could highlight how long it took to build our methodology to improve conversions for e-commerce websites.
IKEA Effect	People tend to place a higher value on things they have created themselves.	Ready-made pancake mix, where you just have to add milk and shake	We could let clients do the website audit themselves using our method. They might be more open to making changes if they find the problems themselves.
Pratfall effect	People who show their imperfections tend to be more trusted.	CXL's marketing training company* ran an ad featuring a testimonial from a student who said, "I had to watch it at 0.25 speed to understand the content," to highlight how advanced it is.	Maybe we don't have to make excuses for taking our time to find ways to increase conversions. We can turn this into a positive thing. We can emphasize that our process takes time because it's the most thorough.

*Louis Grenier. 2024. "Pratfall Effect: How to Use It in Marketing (6 Examples)." *Everyone Hates Marketers.* https://www.everyonehates marketers.com/articles/ pratfall-effect-marketing.

Hopefully, it will give you ideas about what you could do differently for your own **offers**. If you want to go deeper, Table 14.3 features nine core biases that influence human behavior, using the acronym **MINDSPACE**.[76]

Table 14.3. Core Biases Influencing Human Behavior

Core Biases	What It Is
Messenger	We are heavily influenced by who communicates information.
Incentives	Our responses to incentives are shaped by predictable mental shortcuts such as strongly avoiding losses.
Norms	We are strongly influenced by what others do.
Defaults	We "go with the flow" of preset options.
Salience	Our attention is drawn to what is novel and seems relevant to us.
Priming	Subconscious cues often influence our acts.
Affect	Our emotional associations can powerfully shape our actions.
Commitments	We seek to be consistent with our public promises and reciprocate acts.
Ego	We act in ways that make us feel better about ourselves.

76 AG Barr. "Influencing Behaviour Through Public Policy." *Institute for Government.* https://www. bi.team/ wp-content/uploads/2015/07/MINDSPACE.pdf.

TAKE ACTION

Generate unique offer ideas by tapping into cognitive biases.

Here's what to do:

1. **Brainstorm.** For each core bias in Table 14.3, think about how you could improve your current **offers** or develop new ones.

2. **Don't censor yourself.** Write down every idea that comes to mind, even if it seems crazy at first.

Step 3. Let Them Choose Their Own Adventure

This method transforms your offer from a one-size-fits-all to a choose-your-own-adventure. Your **segment** may share similar **struggles**, but how people get there—and how much you help—can vary. I like to think of it as offering different intensity levels, with "intensity" reflecting your level of involvement. The less intense, the more people take the reins.

This is meant to show that the exact same goal can be achieved in many different ways. Two **offers** that target the exact same **struggle** in two different ways may perform differently based on what people expect.

Here's a popular way to come up with **offers** with various levels of intensity:

- **Do-it-yourself (DIY).** You provide the instructions; they put in the work.

- **Done-with-you (DWY).** You offer coaching, support, and guidance along the way.

- **Done-for-you (DFY).** You handle everything; they reap the rewards.

This approach works for anything you sell, whether it's a service or a product. The key is to think beyond the *thing* itself and consider the whole *experience* surrounding it.

Example:

Let's take our East Forged cold brew tea example again. At first glance, it might seem difficult to offer different levels of intensity for something like cans of cold brew tea. But what if we think about the *entire* customer experience?

Remember, we've found out that some customers use East Forged cold brew tea as a substitute for alcohol, a way to treat themselves in the evenings and on weekends. So a done-for-you (DFY) experience could be setting up a stand at night venues and preparing nonalcoholic cocktails using East Forged cold brew tea as the main ingredient.

There are times when people need different levels of intensity. Sometimes I just want to read about a specific topic I'm interested in. I don't want to talk to anyone; I don't want someone to do it for me. Other times, however, it's the opposite. When organizing my brother-in-law's bachelor party, I had absolutely no interest in doing things myself. All I wanted was someone to handle everything for us, from selecting the right cities to go to, curating the activities, and booking the hotels.

By offering different intensity levels, you can cater to a broader range of situations your customers might encounter. Table 14.4 shows how specific situations can be broken down into various levels of intensity.

Table 14.4. Levels of Intensity

	Do-It-Yourself (DIY)	Done-with-You (DWY)	Done-for-You (DFY)
East Forged cold brew tea	Selling cold brew cans online and at makers markets	Offering a booklet full of cocktail ideas for every customer who buys over $100 worth of cans	Setting up a stand at night venues and preparing nonalcoholic cocktails using East Forged cold brew tea as the main ingredient

	Do-It-Yourself (DIY)	Done-with-You (DWY)	Done-for-You (DFY)
Organizing my brother-in-law's bachelor party	Planning and organizing the entire event myself, including choosing activities, booking venues, and coordinating with guests	Hiring a party planner who provides guidance and suggestions, but you make the final decisions and handle some tasks yourself	Hiring a full-service event planning company to handle every aspect of the bachelor party from concept to execution

TAKE ACTION

Transform your offer with varying levels of intensity—how much you do versus how much they do—do-it-yourself (DIY), done-with-you (DWY), and done-for-you (DFY). Here's what to do:

- Think of your current offer as a starting point. How could you tweak it to create "lighter" or more "intense" versions?

- Come up with as many ideas as possible. Don't hold back.

Do-it-yourself (DIY):

- _____

- _____

Done-with-you (DWY):

- _____

- _____

Done-for-you (DFY):

- _____

- _____

Step 4. Reframe the Time Commitment

This method uses a thought-provoking analogy—meditation versus Xanax[77]—in order to improve your offers. Both offer a solution to the same job—relaxation—but their perceived effort and payoff couldn't be more different. The analogy uses a key psychological principle: people are naturally drawn to solutions that appear quick, easy, and instantly gratifying, even if a longer-term solution offers greater benefits.

Think about it. Meditation, while ultimately rewarding, demands consistent effort and patience before reaping its full benefits. It's a slow burn. Xanax, on the other hand, promises (and delivers) near-instant relief with minimal effort. Pop a pill; problem solved (temporarily, at least).

This contrast highlights a crucial point: when we choose between solutions, our perception of effort and time often outweighs reality. A two-hour Netflix binge of your favorite show? Time flies. Two hours of meditation for a newbie? An eternity.

This principle applies to your **offers**. You aim to increase the perceived likelihood of success while minimizing the perceived time delay and effort involved.

---

77 Alex Hormozi. *$100M Offers: How to Make Offers So Good People Feel Stupid Saying No.* Acquisition.com Publishing, 2021.

TAKE ACTION

Here's how to make your offer feel more appealing by reframing its time commitment:

- **Identify the "perceived effort."** Look at your offer's duration, complexity, and required steps from your ideal customers' perspective. What feels daunting?

- **Brainstorm alternative structures.** Can you break it down into smaller, more digestible chunks? Could you offer a condensed version for quicker wins?

- **Emphasize the speed of results.** Instead of focusing solely on the total time commitment and efforts needed, can you think of ways to highlight how quickly they'll start seeing progress?

Step 5. Construct Your Offer Iceberg

The final step is to arrange your offers into what I call an "offer iceberg." This helps prevent overwhelming potential customers and gives you the best chance to make them take action. Why an iceberg? Because icebergs contain no salt water—just pure ice water. And since salt water is slightly heavier, around 87.5 percent of the iceberg stays underwater, while the remaining 12.5 percent shows above the surface.

The same principle applies to your **offers**. The sweet spot is showing just the *hummock*[78]—about 12.5 percent—of what you've got. Why? Because you don't want to overwhelm your **segment**. Aim to keep the tip of your iceberg as sharp, as shiny, and as pointy as possible.

That visible 12.5 percent should be something irresistible. Don't be afraid to start with a free **offer**. It's the classic foot-in-the-door technique. Treat it

---

78 The visible portion or tip of the iceberg is called the "hummock." The portion of an iceberg submerged in water is called the "bummock."

THE OFFERS | 301

as a gift, something you are happy to give away without expecting anything in return. For examples of the offer iceberg in action, see Table 14.5.

Table 14.5. Offer Iceberg in Action

	Tip of the Offer Iceberg (12.5 percent)	Rest of the Offer Iceberg (87.5 percent)	Explanation
LatinUs Beauty Shampoo	"Control" starter kit: 3-ounce travel-size kit containing shampoo, conditioner, and styling cream	"Control" collection with larger bottles Ongoing subscription with a 15 percent saving	A 3-ounce starter kit lets customers discover the products without breaking the bank.
PTDC Online Training	5 Reps Friday—a free email newsletter written by Jon Goodman Free coaching software for online trainers	Self-paced online course with video lessons, digital textbook, and money-back guarantee. One-to-one phone consulting with Jon Goodman	Free newsletter and software are both very generous offers designed to invite trainers into the PTDC's world.
Civet Coffee	"Impress Your Guests" party pack containing coffee samples, brewing gadgets, and a board game	Coffee beans	If civet coffee wasn't so unethical, we could imagine selling a party pack with small tasting samples.

To summarize, you want to show just the hummock (like 12.5 percent) of what you're offering to not freak out potential customers. Keep that visible bit super enticing. Treat it like a teaser. Then slowly unveil the rest of your stuff (87.5 percent). It's all about not overwhelming folks and compelling them to take action.

TAKE ACTION

Create an **offer** iceberg to present your products or services in a way that doesn't overwhelm customers.

Here's what to do:

1. **List all your offers.** Write down everything you can offer customers, from free items to your most premium services.

2. **Identify your "hummock."** Choose one offer that represents about 12.5 percent of your total offerings. This should be:

   ○ Irresistible

   ○ Easy for customers to say yes to

   ○ Possibly free or low-cost

3. **Arrange the rest.** Place your remaining offers (about 87.5 percent) below the surface of your iceberg.

My offer iceberg tip is: _____

The rest of my iceberg includes:

1. _____

2. _____

3. _____

The Doubts: "I Don't Want to Add to the Noise!"

"This type of offer is already very popular in the market, so I don't want to create yet another one that adds to the noise. What should I do?"

We're so hungry to create something different from everything else that we forget to be pragmatic. Don't worry if it seems like everyone is selling an online course, a book, or widget spinners. I see it as a sign that there is good demand. If I had thought that way I would have missed out on so many opportunities by not starting a podcast or this book.

My advice? Harness the demand and then find ways to make your **offer** stand the f*ck out and turn your fear into excitement.

"Will offering free stuff deter people from buying my offers?"

Think of those Michelin Star chefs writing recipe books and cooking on live TV. Are they losing business because they share what they know for free? No. In fact, they're famous *because* they're sharing their knowledge (and not the other way around). Free stuff doesn't diminish what you're worth—it builds trust with your audience.

"What if my offer doesn't work?"

If you have followed everything in this book so far and feel like your **offer** isn't working, there are a few things you can do.

First, you can ask why. Ask the people who have seen your **offer** why they haven't bought it. You can change who it's for, change the way you deliver it, play with the levels of intensity, play with guarantees, play with perceived efforts, and play with cognitive biases. Basically, never, *ever* stop.

"How can I charge for my offer when I feel like I'm not providing a complete solution?"

It's a bit like thinking, "How can this physiotherapist fix the sciatica pain I've had for 18 years in a 30-minute session?" You're reading this book because you know your stuff. The amount of time spent to solve one's **struggles** doesn't matter. Instead, what matters is your ability to help your **segment** make progress.

The Recap: Arctic Ground Squirrel

Your customers are like hibernating Arctic ground squirrels—stuck on autopilot, resistant to change. A great **offer** is your jolt to wake them up. It's not about trickery; it's about presenting a solution so irresistible they are less likely to say no. This chapter is about crafting that irresistible offer, the cherry on top of your hard work.

Let's recap the key takeaways from this chapter:

- **Five steps to build offers that work.** Slice and dice your insights, explore cognitive biases, let them choose their own adventure, reframe the time commitment, and construct your offer iceberg.

- **Don't reinvent the wheel; make it your bitch.** If everyone's doing it (online courses, books, etc.), it probably means there's demand. Harness it; then make your offer stand the f*ck out.

- **Free is your friend.** Giving away free, valuable stuff builds trust and positions you as the expert. Think Michelin Star chefs sharing recipes—it doesn't devalue them; it makes them famous.

- **Offer the iceberg concept:**

  - Hummock (12.5 percent). This is your irresistible, low-friction **offer**.
  - Bummock (87.5 percent). Slowly unveil other **offers**.

- **Is your offer not working?** Ask why! Survey your audience. Show your offer to more people. Tweak it—change the delivery, add guarantees, play with intensity levels, and never stop trying.

The Recap: Continuous Reach

Continuous reach means showing the right message to the right people at the right time, as much as you can afford. This consistent visibility keeps you top-of-mind, so you're more likely to be picked when they're ready to buy. In this stage, we uncovered three additional elements: **triggers, channels, and offers,** as pictured in Figure S.4.1, which was first presented in the introduction to Stage 4 and is shown again here.

Figure S4.1. The last three insights used to reach people.

Let's recap the key takeaways from this stage:

- **Three things make people act.** A **job**, a **struggle**, and a **trigger**. A **trigger** is not a vague "pain point," but a specific event that creates the "boom."

- **Don't be stuck in "communification" mode.** Stop trying to convince everyone and focus on being present where your customers are. Sometimes just being in the right place at the right time is enough.

- **A great offer is your jolt to wake hibernating customers.** It's not about tricking them; it's about understanding them so well it makes it difficult to say no.

To wrap things up, let's put together a **plan for continuous reach.**

PLAN FOR CONTINUOUS REACH

For folks who are *not* ready to buy (future category buyers)

Show up continuously in the right context *without* trying to convince them to buy.

- Invest in **channels** with a "brand-building" objective.
- Focus on **triggers** that take place early in the buying journey.
- Make sure people know your **category**.
- Consistently show your distinctive brand **assets**.

For folks who *are* ready to buy (current category buyers)

Present offers in a way that feels like you're reading their minds.

- Invest in **channels** with a "sales activation" objective.
- Focus on **triggers** that take place late in the buying journey.
- Consistently show your distinctive brand **assets**.
- Show how you solve **ignored struggle(s)** to get the **job** done. Then explain the "cost" of staying with the **alternative(s)**. Then tell them what you are—your **category**—and who you are for—your **segment**. Finally, show them what to do next with an **offer**.

OK, Now What?

By now, I hope the foggy shit has cleared.

Because you *can* stand the f*ck out *without* drowning in marketing bullshit. You *can* stand the f*ck out and have fun in the process. You can stand the f*ck out no matter what curveballs your life (and career) throw at you.

First, you ditched the assumptions you had about your customers by **foraging for insights**. Then you discovered frustrating problems others have overlooked to describe how you're **uniquely positioned** to attract the right people. After that, you developed a **brand that's distinctive**—not *disruptive*—to create an identity that gets noticed, remembered, and liked. And finally, you've put together a plan to **continuously reach** as many of the right people as possible when it's most relevant to them. (See Figure I.4, first presented at the beginning of the book in the Introduction.)

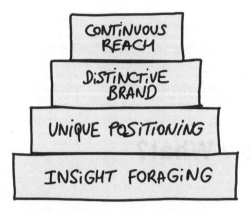

Figure I.4. The four stages of Stand The F*ck Out.

I hope you're proud . . . because I am really proud of you. And I really don't mean it sarcastically.

Before I let you go, I have one last story to share.

You see, the time I struggled most in my career was when I would have an idea, work on it for a few weeks while it was new and exciting, and then abandon it.

Back in 2011 I had a blog called *The Attic of the Web*—my last name, Grenier, means "attic" in French—about entrepreneurship, marketing, and social media (see Figure 1). It wasn't easy to build a blog from scratch back then, so I spent a lot of time on the design, then wrote and published six or seven articles.

Yes, that's it.

Figure 1. My blog's homepage from 2011.

Then I stopped.

A few years later, I moved to Dublin and was interested in starting my own company. I attended a couple of "start-up weekends," where you meet people, come up with an idea on the spot, find a team who wants to develop it with you, and then try to validate it and sell it in one weekend.

I did a couple of them. Nothing ever came of it, and I stopped going.

Then I had a business intelligence project I managed to sell to a company I was interning with. I saw an opportunity in an area where the company struggled and I had an idea to create a new dashboard. The company invested money to help me hire suppliers to build it and I spent months and months developing it without ever showing it to anyone . . . and it failed. No one ever got to use it.

Much of my early adulthood and career was spent in this pattern of feeling excited about my ideas, starting projects, and then dropping them. Why? Probably because I didn't have a map to turn those random bursts of inspiration into something real.

Which brings me to my main point: *anyone* **can read a book like this one, get super excited about the possibilities, and then . . . and then do absolutely fuck all with that knowledge.** I don't want that to happen to you. I want you to stand the f*ck out *for real*—not just in your head. Because doing something that stands the f*ck out is such a thrilling experience. It gets results, it makes you feel good, and it's contagious. Once your clients, your teammates, your boss have experienced it, they will want to live it again and again and again.

I hope you're going to go through this book again whenever you feel like the marketing bullshit is all over your windshield and you struggle to see the road.

Maybe it's a new product you're launching with your team, maybe it's a new business venture you're thinking of launching with your mate from college, or maybe, just like the story of Jon Goodman I shared at the start of the book, it's when the business is in deep trouble and needs rescuing. Whatever it is, while I can't take the wheel for you, I can root for you on the sidelines and encourage you to never, ever fucking give up.

I'm rooting for you; I truly am. You've got this.

Bisous.

Glossary

Term	Definition
Insight	A specific piece of information gleaned directly or indirectly from customers, which gives a nuanced understanding of why customers do what they do.
Poisonous insight	An insight that appears insightful on the surface but leads to harmful consequences, like spending years building something people don't really want.
Job	A specific goal that someone is trying to achieve. It's not about your product or service, but rather the underlying need driving your customers to make progress.
Alternatives	The different paths or solutions available to the people in your **segment** to reach their goal.
Struggles	The obstacles and challenges that prevent the people in your **segment** from making progress.
Irrational struggles	A subset of **struggles** that are emotional and often subconscious, like craving approval, seeking control, or avoiding overwhelm.
Ignored struggle	A subset of **struggles** that alternatives are not solving well—if at all.
Segment	A group of people with similar **ignored struggle(s)** that can be served in a way that gives an advantage against **alternatives**.

Term	Definition
Trigger	An event or a series of events that compel people to act.
Category	The group of things that solve similar **struggle(s)** in a similar way.
Monster	A semi-fictional enemy that represents some of the **struggles** the **segment** is facing.
Point of view (POV)	A set of consistent messages to show you're against the things that harm your audience.
Spices	The actions that bring your **POVs** to life in a way a **segment** will notice.
Assets	The distinctive bits and bobs that make a brand unique. It could be a color, shape, sound, word, or even a mascot.
Channel	A means of meeting potential customers in the context where they experience their **triggers**, compare **alternatives**, and can easily find/buy the **category**.
Offer	A clear, concise proposition that states how you will help people overcome their **struggles** and get the **job** done.

About the Author

LOUIS GRENIER is a recovering Frenchman, failed agency owner, father, husband, contrarian, marketer, and founder of Stand The F*ck Out (STFO). Subscribe to his daily emails here: **stfo.io**.

Did you make it this far? If so, send an email to **louis@stfo.io** with the subject line "I've read this far" and I might send you a little something as a thank you.

Thank you to:

My sassy daughter for inspiring me to enjoy my work every day, and for giving me the drive to finish this book so you could be proud of your dada. I love you.

My wife, Jen, for giving me the greatest gift in the world: our sassy daughter. Thank you for standing by me through all the highs and lows. I love you.

My mémé for passing on her rebellious genes. I miss you every day.

Joe Pulizzi for writing a foreword that stands the f*ck out and picking me up when I was about to quit.

The Tilt Publishing team—Marc Maxhimer and Kristen Moxley—for helping me realize my dream of becoming an author.

Diana De Jesus for joining me on this adventure.

Paul Mellor, Lucy Werner, Sam Conniff, and Jon Goodman for writing lovely comments about my book that I can happily display on the cover.

The mentors who've unknowingly guided me over the last two decades: Adele Revella, Alex Hormozi, Allan Dib, April Dunford, Billy Broas, Blair Enns, Bob Moesta, Borat, Byron Sharp, Dan Ariely, Dave Gerhardt, Dave Harland, David C. Baker, David Darmanin, David Eagleman, Dwight K. Schrute, Eddie Shleyner, Erica Schneider, Eugene Schwartz, Fio Dossetto, Harry Dry, James Clear, Jean Rivière, Jenni Romaniuk, Jim Kalbach, Joanna Wiebe, Joe Glover, Katelyn Bourgoin, Les Binet, Mark Ritson, Marty

Neumeier, Peep Laja, Rand Fishkin, Richard Shotton, Rob Fitzpatrick, Robert Cialdini, Rory Sutherland, Ross Simmonds, Scott Dikkers, Seth Godin, The Daft Punk, Wiemer Snijders, Youngme Moon.

Simone Bruni from Demo Diva, Jon Goodman from the PTDC, A.J. Galante from the Danbury Trashers, César Alejandro Jaramillo from LatinUs Beauty, Sam Conniff from Uncertainty Experts, John Keating from Dark Horse, Florian Heinrichs from client-friendly, Tania Stacey from East Forged, Sarah MacKinnon, and Shanty Baehrel for allowing me to use them as examples throughout the book.

My lovely beta readers who reviewed my unfinished manuscripts and helped transform a mediocre book into one I am truly proud of: Adriana Tica, Alistair Power, Alive Hare, Amy Wright, Andy Bass, Anezka Pavlovicova, Ant Bailey-Grice, Antoine Walter, Caleb Rule, Caroline Shine, Cat Pace, Chloe McDarmont, Diana Porumboiu, Diane Wiredu, Daugirdas Jankus, Edyta Wajda, Erica Conradie, Febriana Isnaini, Hanna Grochocinska, Jason Westgeest, Jessa Nowak, Jocelyn Brady, John Smyth, Jon Dalzell, Jonathan Ross, Jonathan Stark, Katherine Melton-Scott, Kathryn McGarvey, Kelsey Reaves, Kevin Casey, Kevin Sturm, Kieran Cassidy, Laurence Ogé, Lena Weber, Lianna Patch, Liam Wake, Lulah Ellender, Manu Ansoud, Mark Moses, Mathilde Vuillemenot, Melissa Raby, Michael Yeates, Nikita Morell, Pablo Berckmans, Perryn Olson, Phill Agnew, Pierre-Alexandre Schembri, Quentin Heim, R. Dennis Speck, Rob Snyder, Russell Smiley, Sam Gill Murphy, Sian Jones, Vaclav Chmelensky, Veronica Delgado, Vlad Adrian Iancu, Will Slater.

xoxoxo

Louis

L - #0528 - 120225 - C0 - 229/152/18 - PB - DID4402314